T0178802

Enterprise Data Governance

Enterprise Data Governance

Reference & Master Data Management, Semantic Modeling

Pierre Bonnet

First published 2010 in Great Britain and the United States by ISTE Ltd and John Wiley & Sons, Inc.
Adapted and updated from *Management des données de l'entreprise. Master Data Management et modélisation sémantique* published 2009 in France by Hermes Science/Lavoisier © LAVOISIER 2009

ISTE Ltd
27-37 St George's Road
London SW19 4EU
UK

www.iste.co.uk

John Wiley & Sons, Inc.
111 River Street
Hoboken, NJ 07030
USA

www.wiley.com

Library of Congress Cataloging-in-Publication Data

Bonnet, Pierre.
 Enterprise data governance : reference and master data management, semantic modeling / Pierre Bonnet.
  p. cm.
 Includes bibliographical references and index.
 ISBN 978-1-84821-182-7
 1. Data protection. I. Title.
 HF5548.37.B666 2010
 658.4'78--dc22

                                                                    2010014839

British Library Cataloguing-in-Publication Data
A CIP record for this book is available from the British Library
ISBN: 978-1-84821-182-7

Printed and bound in Great Britain by CPI Antony Rowe, Chippenham and Eastbourne.

MIX
Paper from
responsible sources
FSC® C013604
FSC
www.fsc.org

Table of Contents

Testimonials from the
MDM Alliance Group

"Master Data Management and Information Management are key disciplines in any Company Architecture and Service Oriented Architecture initiatives. The MDM Alliance Group is delivering some solid added value in these areas by releasing these procedures in the public domain. Excellent work."

Didier Boulet
Director SOA - THALES Corporate - KTD/Software

"Pierre Bonnet's book on Master Data Management and Semantic modeling is a timely and comprehensive guide to creating solid foundations for Master Data Management within the company. The semantic approach to modeling master data represents an important step toward building industry specific standards and therefore massively reducing the risk and cost of Master Data Management projects. To have Pierre's extensive architectural knowledge and vision within this area in print is a must for anyone embarking on a Master Data Management initiative."

Owen Lewis
Director Product Development - Agile Solutions Ltd

"The data explosion in terms of volume and transactions has crystallized new paradigms such Event Driven Architecture (EDA), Cloud Computing and other models such SaaS. In such a massively distributed environment, completely virtualized and ubiquitous, the quality of data, their localization and transactional integrity will be dramatically critical. Another dimension of business that is magnifying the effect of the vectors described above is the breathtaking acceleration in the swiftness of business change that is forcing companies to rethink the manner in which they manage their critical data and information."

"Rethink it means making a conceptual leap into this new economic model which means that companies will need to be guided in order to successfully achieve their transformation, thus increasing their competitive advantage.

The MDM Alliance Group is an initiative that will guide any company of any size to go through the transition phase in order to reach their goal. The modeling coupled with the semantic approach is an extremely powerful tool to increase the transparency of critical and valuable data while at the same time reducing the complexity of the architecture and multiplicity of interactions. The MDM alliance also provides tools and business templates for accelerating the learning and the operational effectiveness of companies. Bear in mind that data, since the beginning of mankind, has made and broken up empires and, from that view point, nothing has changed except that today data is more important than ever due to the speed of business change, which means that any company must safeguard its highest competitive asset: data."

Didier Mamma
Director EMEA Strategy & Development - Progress Software S.A.S.

"The majority of companies have taken steps towards a better management of their data capital or reference data. They are all looking for reassurance and want to benefit from the thoughts of others.

The MDM Alliance Group therefore brings an essential networking aspect, which is at the base of all good business practice for companies wishing to start a reference based management project. Atos Origin firmly supports the MDM Alliance Group."

Laurent Schapira
BI, CRM & MDM Solutions Manager - Partner Atos Consulting

"The MDM Alliance Group is a debating forum, a *think tank* that prevents us from re-inventing the wheel. The modeling procedures and the ready to use data model help progress from state of the art to the reality of company projects.

The MDM Alliance Group is an accelerator helping to free the players involved be they users in industry or IT. Its contribution to the maturing process in the MDM market is well and truly established."

Clément Roudeix
Director, BI & MDM, Financial Services – SOPRA group

"I have come from a traditional data modeling background where languages were not commonly used, so I have been trying to find some unbiased guidelines that would enable me to express my intentions in a more formal and universal way.

The explanation and examples given within the MDM Alliance Group documents have greatly helped me in this goal. They have enabled me understand just how potentially wide ranging and valuable MDM is."

Graham Chapman
Senior Enterprise Domain Architect: Information Enterprise
Architecture at Inland Revenue, New Zealand

"Time (or money) to market a solution seems to shorten as we age. Should we waste in modeling? Think of the data silos "galaxy" accumulated in less than 20 or 30 years of data processing within your own organization, and ask why? It has been disorganized to such extent because nobody wanted to pay the bill for modeling upfront...so, everybody had to pay anyway, but afterwards (data transformation, data migration, data redesign etc.).

Data (and even more master data) is your asset. It is like your money in the bank. You may not have plenty initially but you most probably want it there for as long as possible. If you leave your safe on weak foundations, you will keep rebuilding and soon discover that everyone around preferred to use the bank as a service instead. Can you still afford to remain alone in your data mastering? Standards bodies like OASIS and others progressively deliver prebuilt vertical models like UBL, CIQ, ACORD, HL7 etc. However, those are intended for data flows and do not fit for data implementation. Packaged solutions (like SAP, Oracle Application, etc.) also provide out-of-the-box configurable data implementation schemas.

However those implementations tend to embed most of your master data (from the package prospective only), thus preventing us from keeping an homogeneous level on data quality, control and governance in the overall IT eco-systems. The same pitfalls apply if your try Corporate Services in SOA before data mastering. This book is a great opportunity for re-using from past experiences and capitalizing on state-of-the-art pragmatic modeling techniques. Beyond is the MAG initiative which is a way to not only avoid the blank page but mostly to provide added value from all of us, as long as we all play the fair game of an open collaborative effort."

Xavier Fournier-Morel
Co-author of the SOA Architecture Guidelines

"MAG is a community Pierre Bonnet founded to share MDM Modeling procedures and pre-built data models. The MDM Alliance Group publishes a set of pre-built data models that include the usual concepts (Location, Asset, Party, Party Relationship, Party Role, Event, Period [Date, Time, Condition]) downloadable from the website. And some more interesting models like Classification (Taxonomy) and Thesaurus organized across three domains.

Although we may disagree about the semantics I do agree with him that adopting this approach can help us avoid setting up siloed master databases...unfortunately often evident when using specific functional approaches such as PIM (Product Information Management) and CDI (Customer Data Integration) modeling."

James Parnitzke-James
James is a hands-on technology executive, trusted partner, advisor, software publisher and widely recognized database management and company architecture thought leader

"The MDM apparatus (it's a lot more than just technologies), is a fundamental component to guarantee that a Company Architecture is translated to an efficient IT system. Moreover, without a correct MDM vision implemented at the four levels (semantic, logical, organizational and technological, see the Praxeme aspects) a

Company Architecture may be a complete failure and a total waste of money. The MAG work (method and pre-built models) is an invaluable step in our search for rationality for the IT system we are building for the near future."

Fabien Villard
Secretary of the Praxeme Institute

"The Praxeme methodology, "Sustainable IT Architecture" and especially Master Data Management have helped me in consulting with various organizations in service-oriented architecture, as well as in implementing the process of IT system overhaul. I recognize the MDM Alliance Group as a precious source of information and exchange platform for methodology."

Jay Zawar
Independent Consultant in SOA

"The correct management of a unique set of data repository is key to the company's agility and financial performance. The MDM Alliance Group clearly demonstrates that this is a business opportunity."

Emmanuel Laignelet
Director of Evolan Solutions – SOPRA Group

"A reference book, that gives new found importance to companies' IT heritage. In this book, Pierre Bonnet answers the concerns of IT architects giving a strong methodological framework for the management of data repository. He puts the data at the heart of the business in perspective and gives an efficient and pragmatic approach resting on a sure-footed base, the corner-stone of business data repositories.

In this book IT architects will find, the keys, a guide in the analysis and structuring in four layers (semantic, pragmatic, logic and software) and a collaborative approach (business/IT) which will help make their first MDM project a '*success story*'".

Olivier Sommerard
Technical Director – KHIPLUS

"Today a large amount of energy is expended to maintain, for better or worse, the quality of data. Whether this be in terms of *data cleansing* or *data integration*. But it is also necessary to take into account from the SOA point of view the wasted effort in the access management to the data. One can only fear that duplications of codes on the lower layers of SOA can only lead to the same in the upper layers.

From the point of view of reference data (data used or produced by several applications), from the moment a drive is made to increase quality and reduce costs, standardization is mandatory. Time and time again this principle has been shown to be true in many industries. Without doubt it is time that the software industry takes into account this standardization at the level of reference and master data management.

The logical consequence of this statement is that we can only wish for the normalization of reference and master data.

In this framework, the processes of the MDM Alliance Group, that is to say the semantic modeling of the MDM and the pre-built data models, will almost certainly become, progressively, a must. An ambitious goal, certainly difficult but promising, being that it offers off-the-shelf models.

Even supposing that these pre-built models cannot be used as they are with our respective IT systems, they do have the advantage of giving us the opportunity to personalize our model without having to start from scratch, an approach which is often costly and reliant on a knowledge base for re-use. The approach certainly merits a trial."

Jean-Pierre Latour
Company Architect – SMALS

"There is an intense worry about the reliability of the KPIs and the reliability of the risk indicators. Because of this, it is not unusual that the same KPI on the one hand supplied from the production data base and on the other from BI do not have the same value. Which one is correct? The explanations by Pierre, on the quality of the data repository and by extension on the quality of operational data are totally convincing: It is possible to correct this state of affairs thanks to MDM. Starting an MDM project is attainable: Both methods and tools exist. Pierre explains them very clearly. It is clear that this work is a contribution that cannot be ignored and which is of great value, to the good management of an MDM project."

Antoine Clave
Information Systems Consultant – FIABILIS

"Master Data Management is a key technology to ensure the consistency and integrity of IT systems. Pierre Bonnet, who is a renowned expert in this field, provides a global view within the company and its IS. In his book "MDM and semantic modeling", he introduces modeling techniques in order to define the best architecture and MDM usage for each IS, thus paving the way to IS maturity improvement."

Philippe Desfray
Director R&D – SOFTEAM

"I have met Pierre Bonnet "virtually" on an MDM-related Linkedin group. This allowed me to discover and join the MAG initiative wholeheartedly. Although a long time database professional (from DBA to Data-base Architect), my exposure to MDM started only a few years ago, with an IBM MDM "draft" solution, while I was involved in "architecting" an analytical DWH model, based on an operational ODS/ETL model, integrating a 3rd party CRM package, and complying with global, corporate wide reporting requirements. My first impression, outside the "siloed" legacy (mainframe) world, was the semantic "chaos" introduced by the brave, new and open, distributed platforms, applications and database management systems. Beyond the versatile XML, the MDM (metadata management) was not standard, not accepted, but even had a lukewarm reception from the majors (IBM, MS & Oracle). It was clear that MDM was something else, a few abstraction layers higher, definitely aimed at the business alignment of the data and application semantics. SOA was hot and it promised relief to IT of all the legacy (mainframe, that is) pains. It is less hot now, but it is more mature and it has become absolutely clear there is no IT alternative to it (sic!).

While becoming an architect (an alliteration for a seasoned systems engineer, with the stress on both terms) entering the marvelous Company Architecture (Zakman's) World I've realized that architects have missed one point: legacy (including new technologies, from MS, Oracle and IBM, among others) was not present explicitly, while (passive) data or (actionable) information were persisted tremendously, all over the place, like in a (flat) Babel Tower. The (world of) IT was (is) flat (courtesy of T. Friedman). The answer to that lack of "dimensions" was (already) there: Master Data Management - that business's own lingua franca, that IT should translate into local platform MDM "dialects", ensuring the long-time aimed "integration" and

xxii   Enterprise Data Governance

"interoperability" of heterogeneous databases and applications.

To my "beginners" experience, Pierre Bonnet has provided the SOA "basics" and he has promised the next and complementary book on MDM "all-you-can-eat". The MDM Alliance Group (MAG) is the "place to be" and to discuss the future and mature MDM, tied to help business to seamlessly integrate and inter-operate data and information. Thank you Pierre!"

Nick Manu
Architect and DBA DB2 zOS & Linux, Crossroad Bank for Social Security, Belgium (eGovernment)

"Pierre is an expert in the MDM domain and understands well the intersection of SOA and MDM which is a rapidly emerging topic in Company Architecture. His work on "Sustainable IT Architecture" is an important contribution to the field. As more companies seek to extract the maximum business value of the existing and ongoing investments in IT, the sustainability model helps to coordinate stakeholders and to establish a higher level of functioning for today's much maligned IT department. The integration of MDM into the SOA conversation reflects a mature understanding of the reality of Company complexity, but also provides a path forward for Architects and Practitioners alike."

Miko Matsumura
Vice President and Deputy CTO at Software AG –
author of *SOA Adoption for Dummies*

"Pierre has delivered, over a few short years, an impressive amount of guidance and best practices, be it with his colleagues at the Praxeme Institute, or by founding the Sustainable IT Architecture and MDM Alliance Group communities.

His vision tackles courageously the problems that IT has been facing for well over a decade now and he is offering an innovative, clear and proven path towards agility. He was one of the first ones to associate SOA and MDM, and more than that to provide a complete articulation between MDM, BPMS and BRMS as part of the Agility Chain Management System."

Jean-Jacques DUBRAY
Co-author of OASIS ebBP, SCA,
Author of SDO Specifications and Composite Software Construction

"An essential step for those who wish to significantly improve (in other words, modernize) the agility of their IT system, the creation of a master data management foundation, an apparently simple issue, can come up against problems which could cause the failure of its implementation. Functional architecture, IS integration (exchanges) modeling..; but also organization around data (governance) and potential added value exploration are some of the elements to be seriously considered once taken on. Through their recommendations, fully shared and added to by Micropole Univers, the MDM Alliance group delivers the Best Practice enabling the try conversion!"

Lilian Jouaud
Director, Company Information Management - Micropole-Univers

Foreword

If Master Data are the DNA of your business, MDM with Data Governance is its genetic engineering.

Why governance of Reference and Master Data must be addressed as a pro-active business initiative and should not be considered as a curative technology project

Reference and master data are the DNA of any organization. They define all the facets of your business and reflect the value and differentiators you provide within the market. Products, customers, channels, locations, geographies, accounts, organization, employees, suppliers, etc., are the critical assets at the heart of your business. The definition of DNA on Wikipedia can easily be applied to reference data: "(DNA) is a nucleic acid that contains the genetic instructions used in the development and functioning of all known living organisms and some viruses. The main role of DNA molecules is the long-term storage of information. DNA is often compared to a set of blueprints or a recipe, or a code, since it contains the instructions needed to construct other components of cells."

As with DNA, reference and master data are the codification of your business, shared across all business lines, consumed by all IT systems.

So, if reference and master data are the DNA of your business, data governance is the genetic engineering. It means that the main purpose of a data governance initiative is to improve the quality, consistency and relevance of this data across the entire organization, not to fix issues after they have already occurred.

As in biology, improving the quality of your data cannot rely only on curative techniques. While data quality and data integration solutions are a key foundation for cleansing and connecting your data, you need to provide your business users with an active control on their shared data. Data governance is a pro-active business initiative that has a real benefit to enabling efficient and effective business initiatives or compliance requirements.

Semantic data modeling and Model-driven MDM

If your goal is to gain a real control over your data, you cannot avoid the data modeling exercise. Without a common and unified description of your data, how could business users share the same concepts?

In this book, Pierre Bonnet introduces the concept of a Model-driven MDM based on semantic data modeling. Far beyond traditional models, semantic models describe your data in meaningful terms for all stakeholders, including business users. This means you can design a rich description of your reference and master data and hide or bypass the usual constraints of IT relational oriented modeling such as join tables or frozen cardinality links. Then it becomes possible to define complex data objects, mix hierarchical, relational and object-oriented concepts, configure business rules and validation controls, add documentation, etc.

Semantic data modeling associated with the Model-driven MDM allows business users to be involved from day one in your data governance program. With a model-driven solution they can easily collaborate on data modeling and quickly achieve a description of their data in their shared business language because "what you model is what you get".

While data modeling requires effort, the realization of a mutual and shared understanding for the whole business will become of recurring importance for a pro-active data governance program. It is the first step to building the best version of the truth and establishing a unique reference and master data repository with active data governance capabilities.

Power to business users

Once data models have been designed, your data governance journey is not over. Building a unique description of your data is useless if business users cannot gain control of data itself. This means that to be active, an MDM/data governance solution must provide not only a central repository for storing the truth, but also a full set of data management features and a user experience for collaboration that maximizes adoption.

Pierre Bonnet proposes an exhaustive description of the core capabilities that business teams need to apply for pro-active governance of their data.

It starts with a rich user experience in order to provide data owners, stewards and managers with a collaborative environment for managing data and improving quality over time. It also addresses key issues such as version control, security, business processes and rules and finally integration of master data across information systems.

Based on his extensive experiences at Orchestra Networks but also the MDM Alliance Group and Sustainable IT Architecture communities, Pierre proposes an unbiased perspective on MDM/data governance methodology, in order to help you build a truly pro-active data governance program.

Christophe Barriolade
CEO, Orchestra Networks

Preface

Drastic reduction of IT budgets, even more so in this time of economic crisis, signifies a lack of understanding as to IT's strategic contribution to business. This perception is changing with the success of newcomers that are acting with modern IT infrastructures such as Dell, Amazon, Google, Facebook, etc. It is also changing because the restrictions of legacy IT architecture are becoming too much to cope with, faced with the requirements of information traceability, essential for mastering risks in modern and complex organizations.

Poor knowledge of and lack of auditability of data, business rules and processes block business users' understanding of IT, which reduces the strategic interest that they should have for it. In a world where IT has a key role in the execution of processes and in the exchange of information, a company that gives up faced with this opacity takes a considerable operational risk, that of the loss of control over its activity. To avoid this, new methods and techniques exist in order to progressively transform IT systems and improve their transparency.

This change of direction runs deep. An information system, handicapped by a rigid IT, can liberate itself from it. A new IT pact is born from this transformation approach. It places the true value of the information system outside software which is often locked in, hard-coded and stratified, in order to situate it in a new kind of information system assets repository, under the responsibility of business users themselves. The first of these repositories is that of reference and master data, i.e. through Master Data Management (MDM).

The loss of control of data

Under pressure, to be ever more agile and conform to business regulations[1], a company can no longer tolerate a rigid IT: it must find the means to transform it in order to make it more flexible and transparent for business users. This transformation starts by retaking control of the heart of systems, that is to say the data, in a unified manner across the whole of the information system. The renovation of IT cannot be achieved while the meaning and value of data are unreliable and not shared by the actors in the company. This re-appropriation effort is even more urgent as IT is not only unsuitable for business users, it also lacks transparency for IT specialists themselves, even though they are in charge of maintaining it. They no longer know the data they are supposed to govern well enough. It is too often situated in legacy databases which are poorly documented.

Like me, the reader will have been confronted, too often, with the inability of a company to provide up to date documentation of the meaning of data, beyond a technical description. This lack of quality is costly and poses strategic problems that have been studied by a number of consulting firms such as, for example, here: "Companies are making bad operational decisions every day of the week [and losing money] because of bad data quality", says Ted Friedman, an analyst at Gartner Inc. in Stamford, Connecticut. "Poor data management is costing global businesses more than $1.4

---

1. Sarbanes-Oxley Act (SOX), Basel II, Solvency II, Green regulations, etc.

billion per year in billing, accounting and inventory, according to a survey of 599 companies by PriceWaterhouseCoopers in New York" [BET 01].

This lack of control is accelerated because a company inherits the systems that integrate with new ones, which there are increasingly more of and which are spread out. They must also interact with others under the control of partners, clients, providers, etc. Consequently, there are multiple information exchanges between databases and their quality is strategic to support the reliability of processes. To manage these exchanges, IT often has at its disposal technical integration solutions[2] which, unfortunately, often lack sufficient modeling. Since the beginning of the 1990s, these solutions have been used in a technical manner, without taking into account data modeling. The consequences of this are an increase in the complexity of integration software and poor data exchange quality. Most of the time, no reliable documentation exists on their validation rules. They are locked and scattered in the software, without being open enough to the business itself. To restore reliability of exchanges, it is necessary to provide a data model which can be understood by business users and which they can profit from in order to improve data validation rules.

Data repositories

It is in this context, of worrying about the quality of IT systems, that data modeling is taking the front of the stage, after several years of being abandoned. In particular, reference and master data (that which is shared by a large number of functions in the company) are the objects of particular attention. They are often filed under the term

---

2. EAI: Enterprise Application Integration; ESB: Enterprise Service Bus; ETL: Extract-Transform-Load.

"data repositories". This data is strategic, as it supports the quality of business process by providing reference and master information: pricing, typology of clients, product description, organization description, financial structures, regulatory conditions, etc. The patrimonial value of this data is significant, as the transformation of systems is achieved by regaining control over it.

To leverage this heritage, it is necessary to reactivate data modeling techniques which have been known for some time and modernize them to take into account new agility and system transparency requirements. We will see how to act in stages, by preserving what is already in place and then beginning a progressive transformation of information systems. This approach is based on Master Data Management (MDM) and will make apparent the heritage value of reference and master data that becomes available to business users.

An MDM system resembles a data storage facility, like a data warehouse in a business intelligence domain. However, it is quite different in that it manages detailed and synchronized data, in real time if necessary, with the rest of the information system. MDM brings data governance functions which are not present in business intelligence systems: data archiving, version management, screen for data authoring depending on the use contexts such as languages or multi-channel, auditability or many others that we will discover here.

Objective of this book

This book is intended for all the actors in charge of information systems and involved in the transformation of IT in order to improve its transparency.

General management must perceive the strategic benefits of reference and master data governance functions. The discovery of the patrimonial value of data is at the center of any financial analysis of the MDM approach. The traceability of reference and master data is strategic to reinforce the alignment of the company with business regulations and allows it to better follow its risks.

Business users must take hold of MDM systems in order to re-appropriate their reference and master data, in a reliable and secure manner, in collaboration with the IT department. The technical tools and office automation tools which are limited to an approximate management of reference and master data, are replaced by an MDM system, on the basis of a rich data model shared by the whole company and an organization which is adapted to it.

IT professionals must assimilate the procedures of data modeling and help their business users to use them. They must take into account the essential work of integrating the MDM system with the rest of the information system, which changes the way in which the implementation of EAI/ESB solutions are approached.

We hope that universities and schools, which form the next generation of managers and IT professionals, will profit from this book to relaunch the discipline of modeling. Training courses have put an exaggerated importance on the techniques of object oriented programming, leaving behind certain fundamentals of IT, and modeling in particular. It is essential to return to this; this book has the aim of demonstrating the reasons why this is so urgent and how to answer it, in particular for reference and master data.

How to use this book

We have organized the book so that the reader can benefit from it depending on whether he or she belongs to general management, to other company staff, or to the IT Department:

– for stakeholders, Part One, The MDM Approach, places data repository management in the strategic approach of the financial valuation of the intangible assets of an IT system. The tools and procedures for this valuation help the company to better align with business regulations and increase the transparency of data for business;

– for business units, Part Two, MDM from a Business Perspective, details the operational contribution of the data governance functions and deals with organizational aspects of the MDM approach;

– for IT management, Part Three, MDM from the IT Department Perspective, presents the modeling of data repositories. These procedures are founded on sustainable building blocks for data repositories and key concepts: separation of concerns, rich data models, business object lifecycles, Enterprise Data Architecture, and loose coupling of data. This part also details the technical integration of an MDM system with the rest of a company's IT systems.

Any reader who is anxious to understand the outline of semantic modeling can, at any time, go directly to Chapter 8 "The Semantic Modeling Framework". Even though this is technically advanced, this chapter must nonetheless be carefully studied by all actors in charge of information systems.

The success of the MDM approach depends on the quality of semantic data modeling. Even though this modeling concerns IT and business users, putting it into practice requires a high level of technical know-how, which means that we will go into it in more detail in the section dedicated to the IT department.

Guide to reading the book

The introduction summarizes the definition of the MDM system in order to provide the essential reference points for reading the book.

Part One allows an approach to MDM from a strategic and financial perspective:

– Chapter 1, *A Company and its Data*, sets out the report of the current situation in terms of data repository management. We present definitions of reference/master data and the most frequent types of data repository (CDI, PIM-PLM, LDAP) compared to the MDM approach;

– Chapter 2, *Strategic Aspects*, places the MDM system as a pre-requisite for the progressive transformation of information systems. We see how the principle of the system agility chain[3] acts as a motor for this transformation;

– Chapter 3, *Taking Software Packages into Account*, is concerned with the application of MDM systems to software packages. We present the criteria for choosing software packages which enable high standards in the MDM approach;

– Chapter 4, *Return on Investment*, brings together elements for the financial evaluation of the MDM system: quality and reliability of data, better control of operational risks, and the transformation value of the IS.

---

3. A.k.a. Agility Chain Management System (ACMS).

Part 1 – The MDM Approach	Part 2 – MDM from a Business Perspective
Chapter 1 A company and its data	Chapter 5 MDM maturity levels and Model-driven MDM
Chapter 2 Strategic aspects	Chapter 6 Data governance functions
Chapter 3 Taking into account software packages	Chapter 7 Organizational aspects
Chapter 4 Return on investment	

Part 3 – MDM from the IT Department Perspective	
Chapter 8 The semantic modeling framework	Chapter 11 Organization modeling
Chapter 9 Semantic modeling procedures	Chapter 12 Technical Integration of the MDM system
Chapter 10 Logical data modeling	

Part Two presents what the MDM brings to business:

– Chapter 5 presents *MDM Maturity Levels and Model-driven MDM* which extends from virtual MDM to semantic MDM via static MDM, the risks of which we highlight;

– Chapter 6, *Governance Functions*, lists the necessary functions in order to govern reference and master data: version management, data entry depending on use contexts, data validation rules, data approval process, etc.;

– Chapter 7 describes the *Organizational Aspects* that must be taken into account in order to produce a successful data model across the whole of a company. It also details the necessary roles for reference and master data governance (data steward, data owner, etc.).

Part Three presents the methods and techniques that an IT department must master in order to deploy an MDM system:

– Chapter 8, *The Semantic Modeling Framework*, details the semantic modeling objectives, their foundations and methods for a company to succeed at this modeling, indispensable for MDM;

– Chapter 9 presents *Semantic Modeling Procedures* for the construction of a sustainable and rich data model, independent of an organization, capable of absorbing evolutions and offering a foundation of the IS transformation;

– Chapter 10, *Logical Data Modeling*, presents the procedures for logical modeling applied to reference and master data: loose coupling of data and derivation into the storage techniques used by the MDM system;

– Chapter 11 presents procedures for *Organization Modeling*, i.e. data approval processes (workflows) and use cases as well as their derivation into the logical model;

– Chapter 12, *Technical Integration of an MDM system*, details the technical integration of the repository with the rest of the IT system. It gives reference points for decision-making under the control of IT architects.

Acknowledgements

I would like to thank everyone who helped me with the re-reading and improvement of this book, especially Christophe Barriolade, Paul Billingham, Jean-Jacques Dubray, Mickaël Chevalier, William El Kaim, Olivier Maturin, Manuel Sajus, Fabien Villard and all the editors of the testimonials for the MDM Alliance Group.

This book would not have been possible without the considerable support of Dominique Vauquier, the main author of the Praxeme method. I thank Dominique for his support of my work over the years and his unparalleled contribution to the field of semantic modeling.

Thank you also to all those involved in the MDM Alliance Group community. This book is dedicated to them.

Introduction to MDM

Did you know that in every IT system there is a lot of data with values which do not depend on the execution of transactions supporting the company's activity? Nonetheless, that data is no less strategic as it is used as reference and master data during the execution of the transactions. If this data is flawed, then the value chain is put in jeopardy, sometimes dramatically. Examples include the description of products and services, the organizational structures of a company, the definition of a financial flow classification required by business regulations, the customers' descriptions and other third parties, etc.

Do you know how this reference and master data is managed from an IT point of view? In most companies, the data is governed with heterogenous tools and processes, which lead to serious quality and traceability problems: mistakes in product price, in configuration of a service, lack of traceability surrounding the classification of financial flow, inaccurate alignment of commercial transactions with business regulations (that nonetheless need to be respected), inability to access a reliable data history, tools which are too technical and heterogenous for reference and master data entry and consultation.

This data constitutes a common fountain of knowledge with considerable value. It is an actual asset, the financial assessment of which should be a significant advantage in launching an information system transformation to reduce the opacity of IT. The richness of the information system is less in its transaction execution devices and more in its reference and master data that enables its realization. The computerization of transactions is just a tooling that must conform to requirements; it is almost a commodity. By contrast, the reference and master data is information with high added value; it is the base of knowledge without which the company would have no value. We can automate transactions in an Enterprise Resource Planning (ERP) software package or delegate them to a contractor, but a company cannot do without its reference and master data. A commercial brand such as Pepsi has a financial value; reference and master data answers to a similar valuation mechanism, applied to the immaterial assets of the information system itself.

I.1. Principal characteristics of MDM

Master Data Management[1] is an approach concerned with reference and master data in order to guarantee their unified governance under the control of business users. This book is dedicated to explaining this approach and we will return to the following principal characteristics:

– MDM is a warehouse of reference and master data that provides a business tool for data authoring and consultation. It offers high added value functions enabling the management of versions, auditability, rights

---

1. It is difficult to determine with certainty who came up with the term MDM, its use being so widespread from the moment it appeared. It is probable that one of the founding texts is that of Rohm & Hass: *Laying the Groundwork for ERP: The Story Behind the Company's Master Data*, July 2002 [ROH 02].

management, etc. This warehouse is managed, from a logical point of view, in manner which is unified for all of the information system, even though its technical architecture can be distributed;

– MDM is based on a model that describes reference and master data and details its meaning, relationship and validation rules to apply to updates. This model is shared across the entire company; it is valid for the whole scope of the information system and for the entirety of transactions. It is not a technical model. It is a semantic data model of knowledge that describes the reference and master data with precision. To obtain this model, it is necessary to adopt a semantic modeling approach;

– MDM is a software package. It must be able to take into account any semantic data model in order to automatically make available all data governance functions. This tool is used by business teams in charge of the management of reference and master data, or teams interested in data querying. This business orientation places the functions of this tool beyond technical data administration, profiting a real reference and master data governance. Business users assume operational responsibilities themselves, including data entry, managing rights, creating versions of data, having autonomous access to the audit trail, etc. IT experts still need to be involved but at the discretion of business users who decide the delegation levels of data governance that they wish to share.

I.2. Beyond MDM

The implementation of a reference and master data repository is the first stage in the transformation of IT. However, the assets of the information system are not limited to these data. It is necessary to pursue the same strategy of transparency improvement by profiting from two other repositories. The first of these acts on business rules and is based on the *Business Rules Management System* (BRMS) approach. The second acts on the processes and is based on the *Business Process Management* (BPM) approach. We will see that the order of implementation of these repositories follows an indisputable logic: it is first necessary to regain possession of reference and master data, and then act on business rules in order to retake control of the processes. Unfortunately, too many companies adopt an approach based around processes at the start, leaving aside the aspect of regaining control of data and its rules; this is a considerable failure of IT.

The MDM approach is situated in this dynamic of the re-appropriation of data, rules and, finally, processes. MDM is not uniquely applied to answer data governance needs. It must act as a sustainable foundation at the time of the addition of rules and processes repositories. If the MDM design fails, it cannot fulfill this role and the improvement of the transparency of the information system is incomplete.

PART ONE

The MDM Approach

Chapter 1

A Company and its Data

This first chapter is dedicated to the role of data governance within companies and will enable us to make a clear definition of it. We will also see how the most commonly used data repository tools such as Customer Data Integration, Product Information Management, and structure and organization directories fit into the context of the MDM approach.

1.1. The importance of data and rules repositories

Master data management is not solely limited to the IT community. It is not only about rationalizing reference and master data, increasing their quality nor even laying the groundwork or preparing the first steps for a possible transformation of IT systems. These are important objectives but are insufficient to place MDM in its proper context.

To understand the true impact of MDM, it is important to consider the asset value of an IT system. Indeed, it is a crucial factor in the strategic and financial evaluation of the MDM approach. In order to get a sense of the outline of this assessment and its relationship with data management, here is a real story taken from a conversation with the head of IT systems of a large industrial company. This CIO was explaining to me that his IT systems were performing well, all the production KPIs were good, with a good capacity to respond to the needs of the business thanks to centralized operations and fixed price outsourcing, based on certified quality procedures. The contribution of IT to the quality of the system was a sure thing in the mind of this CIO, who was convinced of its success. Very impressed by this viewpoint, I wanted to find out more:

"How can you measure this contribution?", I asked.

"I put an IT management control system in place that measures the global costs for each project. At the start of the project we sign a contract with our users that covers the commitments in terms of planning and return on investment", answered the CIO.

"You are the director of IS and IT systems. Do you not find it odd that your management control, i.e. your P&L (Profit and Loss) does not correspond with your function?"

"What do you mean?" He asked, surprised.

"Instead of only having an IT management control, you should have an IS management control, in agreement with your role as head of IS and IT systems. If you measured the costs, the planning, and the rate of IT return you would not be as convinced as to your contribution to the IS and IT system. Truth be told, you have no indicators to prove this."

"I don't understand? What should I be measuring?"

"Your assets! What are they?", I insisted.

"We have computer hardware, software licenses, subcontracts and operating contracts. We already take those into account in our management control."

"And what about your software and your databases? They represent a fountain of knowledge of the company's processes. These pieces of software embody the Information System, especially as your IT systems support all the company's processes. There are, without a doubt, no decisions or operations without the support of computers as a tool. Do you realize the importance of this and do you know how to measure it?"

"No. How could we measure it? It's impossible."

"If you cannot evaluate it, then you will not be able to measure the impact of IT on the Information System. You are not in a position to do it because the capital asset value of the Information System, the one that you should find out, is trapped in IT systems that are not readily accessible to the business, in programming languages and databases only understood by your IT experts. At best, only a part of the IS assets are known via reporting tools, business intelligence tools and workflows for certain business processes."

"And how could it be otherwise?"

"By putting together another IT system. You need to get the IS assets out of your software. Among these assets, it is important to first consider the reference and master data. You need a solution enabling business users to take control of their reference and master data, via a unified tool applied across the whole of your IT system, and with governance functions allowing the business users to enhance this data, depending on the version and use contexts (country, organization, etc.), querying and auditing them, and rating their reliability. This concerns very large domains of data, ranging from product and service descriptions to business regulatory configurations. Its financial value is estimated using tools such as benchmarking. For example, at the time of a takeover by another company, your company would be in a position to compare its data repository for product configuration with that of the targeted company. The same comparison is possible with other data repositories such as business regulations, accounting and financial structures, etc. The value of the data repositories is thus concrete. The method to obtain such a goal exists and the MDM approach is the first step."

"That's a radical break!"

"Yes, similar to the passage from the light bulb to the transistor! After having taken into account the asset value of the reference and master data, you have a similar approach to business rules with a BRMS (Business Rules Management System) and with BPM (Business Process Management). Your IS and IT management control can therefore be enhanced with an inventory of assets in terms of reference and master data, business rules and processes. Thus it changes into management accounting of the whole IS and IT system. It is from then on, and not before, that you can evaluate the relevance of the IT in terms of its contribution to the IS and its alignment with the business. The lower your asset inventory is, the more blurred your vision of the situation is. With no assets to evaluate, you are running blind!"

Before reaching this stage of maturity, at which you will be able to incorporate business repositories into management control, you must first sort out the data repositories, in other words establish an MDM system. To do so, you have to return to the basics of IT.

1.2. Back to basics

These past few years, innovation in IT has not left much room for database reconstruction.

Most of the initiatives in the object oriented approach and Java development, of BPM and even Service Oriented

Architecture (SOA) were carried out taking into account legacy databases without restructuring them. Companies did not have the means nor the objective to modify these databases. The IT industry[1] has largely maintained the idea that new technologies would be capable of offering a return on investment without modifying the core of existing systems. Now, companies are realizing that these new technologies have been oversold. It is now obvious but it was not easy to convince people that, if data is no longer reliable, then the software that use them are also no longer reliable, whether they be oriented objects, BPM, SOA or others.

During the past few years, there has been a steady decline in the quality of data and data modeling expertise is becoming increasingly rare. It is more common to hire a Java engineer than a UML data modeler. It is even present in computer science training courses, surely a sign that this decline runs deep. And yet, in the first days of IT, a formal approach to data existed. Procedures and methodology were set in stone with[2]:

– conceptual data modeling to present business information in a format that can be understood by people who are not technical specialists;

– logical data modeling for the translation of conceptual modeling to data structures that respect IT needs and feasibility;

– physical data modeling for the translation of logical modeling into software, i.e. the "physical database schema".

---

1. Software vendors, consulting groups, IT services companies, etc.
2. This terminology was incarnated in the MERISE methodology in France, from the 1970s. The same levels appear in several English language approaches that have been around for some time, in particular the Zachman Framework from about the middle of the 1980s.

IT experts concerned themselves with establishing models that had a life expectancy that was not that of the processing. Relational algebra, and its translation to normal forms, has contributed to the quality of data models[3]. This strict modeling has given birth to databases placed at the heart of IT systems, giving greater stability and, once again has been widely exploited by companies. The organization of an IT Department left room for data administration. This administration was not only concerned with technical models; it was also concerned with business models, supported by semantic data dictionaries. Data administrators, a valid role within an IT Department, bring together the knowledge of these models (conceptual, logical) in order to pool modeling resources and favor further re-use. These administrators interested themselves in all types of data, from reference and master data (i.e. those shared by application systems) to transactional data.

Today, few organizations have maintained data administration at the business model level. For the most part, they have been lost in a technical database administration, necessary but insufficient to guarantee the durability of business models.

The addition of tactical databases around the heart of an IT system, but also the silo approach and software packages, has led to a fragmented architecture and poor documentation of data. Contemporary IT has not been able to completely preserve its database heritage.

---

3. The normal form applies to a group of data which forms a class, an entity or even a table depending on the vocabulary used. In the 1st normal form, each data element is atomic (at its lowest level). In the 2nd normal form, a data element depends on the whole of the primary key and not a part. In the 3rd normal form, all the data that does not belong to the primary key is not dependent on a non-key data element. The normal form is cumulative and allows us to avoid functional data dependency.

Additionally, new concepts such as agility and traceability of information are needed that did not exist with the same intensity/degree of importance at the time. It is important to understand past differences in order to act more appropriately now.

1.2.1. *Past differences*

How do we reclaim data when IT heritage stems from many decades of hard-coded software developments and the use of software packages?

Taking a new approach to a data model across the whole of a company, avoiding the big-bang effect, valid for all the functional and technical IS silos, as well as data exchanges with partners, is an unachievable task in a single step.

In contrast with the early periods of IT (1960–1980), we are now facing a legacy that needs to be reformed. This is a situation that IT experts do not like, as they are keen to keep their legacy software. It is harder to take away a piece of software than to add one.

Furthermore, the IT industry is facing a not only generational but technical regeneration:

– IT professionals who had the first experience of database modeling across the whole of an IS during the 1970s, are now, increasingly, retiring. And with them, the know-how of data modeling is disappearing;

– during the past 20 years, techniques have dramatically evolved, and mastering them is essential in order to elevate the responsiveness of a system. It is especially important to benefit from object oriented approaches, standards such as XML schema and Model

Driven Architecture[4]. The feedback and lessons learned to carry out such a change are missing, even though the methods and tools are ready to be exploited.

It is indeed a transformation and not simply an addition of further layers of software to that which are already in place, which would only complicate the situation. The ability of the existing systems to take on an extra layer of complexity is coming to a stage which companies should not exceed. The risk of overdosing on complexity could lead to the loss of control of an Information System through its data.

The first step in order to improve the situation without starting all over again is to regain control of data, without imposing modifications on in-house software or software packages already in place. It is all about reference and master data, i.e. data shared and initialized before use by transactional systems. This could be, for instance, configuration of products, structures and organization descriptions, or financial classifications etc. And this is where the MDM approach comes in.

The improvement in management of this data, be it reference or master data, is also necessary in order to meet new business regulations such as Sarbanes Oxley, Basel II, Solvency II, etc. These regulations require a very high level of auditability and traceability in terms of information use.

This reactivation of data modeling comes with the incorporation of new business requirements and technological innovations:

   –   reference and master data governance should not only be the responsibility of IT. Business users must be allowed to govern data, in terms of management rights, data entry, version management, queries, etc.;

---

4. In the sense of the standard Model Driven Architecture (MDA) of the Object Management Group (OMG).

– the methodological and technical innovations of these past few years, especially the object oriented approach, process management, SOA and standards such as XML should be made available to build rich data models, enabling the automatic software generation of data administration functions. This administration, as well as being business-oriented and aligned with models, is re-named Data Governance.

1.2.2. *The rich data model*

The definition of a data element requires information that goes well beyond the description of its attributes (such as its name, its format or its owner) that are often found in an approach involving a data dictionary only. It is also important to describe its relation to other data. The meaning of the data is revealed by its associations with others. It is not just about creating a data dictionary but a model that expresses the relationships between the information in a holistic fashion. Philip Howard of *Bloor Research* dedicates a entire study in his report entitled "Data Discovery" and notes that "we believe that the ability to discover and understand the relationships that exist across your data, wherever it resides, is of fundamental importance to a number of IT disciplines" [HOW 09]. For instance, a product is linked to factories that ensure its assembly and that product is also linked to commercial entities that are involved in its distribution. Depending on whether the products are the responsibility of the headquarters or of affiliate organizations, factories and commercial units can differ. It relates to a validation which depends on the use context in which the data is used: either by Head Office or by affiliates. Therefore the relationships between the data reveal validation rules that are vital to the MDM approach. They are used by the repository to control the integrity of the data.

It would be best to include or make clear these rules in data models[5]. We therefore avoid the risks associated with an approximate modeling that has to be completed by specifications found outside the models which are hard to maintain and understand. This is the reason why rich data models are needed. It is not just about a static description of information. Modeling also takes into account a dynamic description of the data, i.e. the validation rules, the behavior of associations depending on the use contexts and the lifecycles of the business objects. In order to obtain this model, we will see that semantic modeling[6] procedures must be applied.

1.3. Reference/Master data definition

There is no standard definition for reference and master data, although attempts have already been made, such as:

– "Among all data, some is more critical for the business activity and the IT system as they are for the most part shared between a number of applications: we shall call it reference and master data" [REG 08];

– "Sometimes called reference data, master data consist of facts that define a business entity – facts that may be used to model one or more definitions or views of an entity. Entity definitions based on master data provide business consistency and data integrity when multiple IT systems across an organization (or beyond) identify the same entity differently" [RUS 08];

---

5. Simple rules are directly included in the data model; the more complex rules are declared and their implementation is based, for preference, on a business rules management system.
6. These are described in detail in the last part of this book. They are not familiar to the management world, nor to business practice. Nonetheless, we strongly recommend a careful reading of Chapter 8 to acquire the basis for this new approach of the formalization of knowledge.

– "Master data is simply the data associated with core business entities such as customer, employee, supplier, product, partner, asset, etc. This data can reside in many different systems. For example, customer data may reside in a sales force automation system, an e-commerce system, a marketing system, a billing system and a distribution system. Equally, product data may reside in product development systems, manufacturing systems, planning systems and storage systems. A trait of master data, therefore, is that subsets of it are needed in multiple systems to control the continuity of business operations as processes progress throughout the enterprise." [FER 08].

We will give our definition based on the fact that data falls into the category of reference and master data in one of the following situations:

– data is initialized and updated before use by transaction systems;

– data is duplicated across multiple systems. This frequent situation opens up the scope of use for the reference and master data widely;

– data is exchanged with third parties situated outside the limits of the company's IT system.

An MDM system unites the governance functions of this data and makes them accessible for business users. It is based on a unified data model, valid in the following three situations: the same piece of data can be validated before use by transactional systems, it can be duplicated in multiple databases, and exchanged with third parties, all at the same time.

Unification of the repository

MDM brings with it a unified and centralized management of reference and master data. This does not mean that the physical architecture must be centralized. It is possible to opt for a distributed technical architecture. We will return to this IT aspect in Chapter 12.

1.3.1. *Data initialized before use by transactional systems*

Each data initialized before its use by the transactions that support the company processes, is a reference or master data. This data is often administered by heterogenous, technical and sometimes even simple automated office tools (such as spreadsheets). They are employed by teams responsible for the functional and IT parameter settings.

The structure of this data can be simple (this is often the case with codes and labels). This is reference data. More complex data is also involved, associated with validation rules and integrity constraints. This is the case for instance with product configurations, organization definitions, charts of accounts, etc. This is master data.

For these types of data, an MDM system replaces the existing technical and heterogenous tools. It brings a unified business data governance, across the whole of the Information System, with high value added functions such as version management, data input by use contexts, data traceability, etc.

1.3.2. *Duplicate data*

When a data element is duplicated in multiple systems, update synchronizations must be dealt with. The data must have the same value in all of its storage zones. In order to solve this problem, IT integration solutions need to be put into place, with particular focus on data transport between systems (EAI/ESB/ETL).

Most of the time, these data exchanges do not sufficiently take into account the rules of validation and the referential integrity constraints that link the data together. It is therefore necessary, in parallel with these data exchanges, to develop complementary software to control these flows during their transport.

Due to the fact that this processing is not described in the data model, an added complexity arises in the software which penalizes the transparency of these data exchanges: everything that is not expressed in the data model is the object of hard-coded programming in the integration software.

The duplication of data also generates duplication of its validation rules. For instance, for the same data update, it is not uncommon to have validation rules in the system that are at the origin of the modification, as well as in the integration layer (EAI/ESB/ETL) and in the target systems. From then on, it is impossible to guarantee that these validation rules all compatible with one another. This can lead to a situation where one system accepts a data modification and another rejects it and keeps the old value. A validation gap can then appear in the IT system. This is a sure source of low quality.

IT architects have a solution to avoid this gap. They try and put a distributed transaction mechanism in place: if one of the systems refuses the modification, then all refuse it. Sadly, this mechanism is very complex and greatly affects the responsiveness of IT. It is better to avoid it. Indeed, the cost of the implementation of a two-phase commit technology and/or a specific software development for dealing with the distributed transaction is often too expensive.

Whatever the case, it becomes difficult to distinguish between systems that accept data and those that do not, as there is no unified data repository, nor any common validation rules.

These validation rules become complex when referential integrity constraints that extend over multiple databases within the IS come into play. For instance (see Figure 1.1): "a *product* (Database No. 1) is only created if the *factory code* (Database No. 2) which it is affiliated with is under the management of an *organization* (Database No. 3) that has an ongoing production *agreement* (Database No. 4) with the *company* or one of its *partners* (Database No. 5), that has been active for the past twelve months, at its disposal".

In a scattered IT system, under the influence of multiple databases that have to be synchronized, it is difficult to decide where these referential integrity constraints should be set up. Often, in the absence of a better method, they are found in several places in silos and hard-coded in the integration layer. With the complexity that arises with the enforcement of these types of rules, a company is heading for disaster. It is not the complexity that is at fault, but rather the way in which these rules are handled.

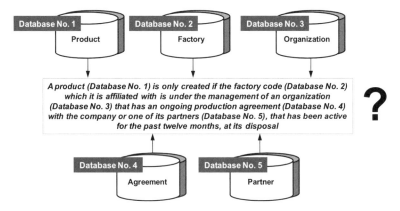

Figure 1.1. *Referential integrity constraints spread over several databases*

Finally, a scattered IT system, under the influence of data duplications, is an unrecognizable system. Knowledge of the data and their relationships is diluted at several points in such an Information System, and only the data integration layer is at hand in order to try and achieve some unified data validation. This is misleading, however, because this integration is not based on a real data model in the traditional sense. It remains technical (pivot format), without transparency, vis-à-vis the business users who should be more involved in the management of the necessary validation rules.

In order to rectify this situation, it is important to have a data repository that is used by the integration layer. This data repository embodies a data model that jointly expresses the content of business objects used by data exchanges between systems, as well as the totality of their validation rules and their relationships with one another (referential integrity constraints). This is a rich data model.

This data repository is accompanied by governance functions that enable data to be queried, using business friendly terms, to access audit trails and data traceability. These functions enable successive versions of objects to be stored in order to follow data exchanges over time, compare versions of the same object, or to restart a process of data synchronization at a known version, etc.

These functions are not just at the disposal of IT experts, as this is not an additional technical supervision console. On the contrary, it is a tool designed for business users (see Figure 1.2).

This data repository is an MDM system used for the range of data duplicated between systems. The data in question can be a reference or master data (codes, parameters, organization description, product description, etc.) but also transactional data (turnover, stock level, bonus, etc.). This is an "MDM for data flows".

This approach makes transactional data eligible for the governance functions offered by MDM, as soon as it is the object of a duplication and data exchanges between systems.

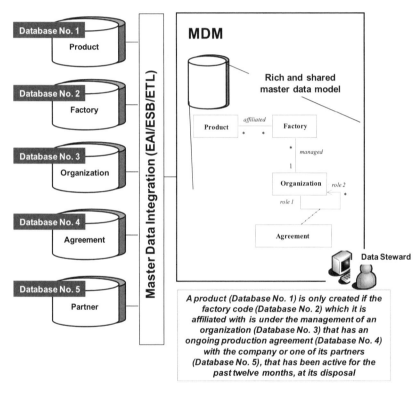

Figure 1.2. *Unified management of referential integrity constraints*

Data repository for business intelligence

> Business intelligence repositories[7] also take advantage
> of the MDM to obtain, reliably, at the same time not
> only the reference and master data but also the up-to-
> date values of the transactional data duplicated in the
> different silos.

1.3.3. *Data exchanged with third parties*

The data exchanged outside an IT system needs to have
an infallible traceability. In the case of legal issues arising
over the quality of data exchanged with third parties, one
must be able to find evidence that the data have been sent.
This traceability cannot only be satisfied by technical data
logging because the data is interlinked, changes value over
time, can be subject to different initializations depending on
the third party, or be subject to version management, etc. A
data repository applied to data exchanges is needed,
identical to the one already described for data duplication,
associated with governance functions enabling all of the data
exchange to be consulted, in a secure manner. In other
words, this is an MDM system and each data flow exchanged
with third parties is also managed as master data.

1.4. Searching for data quality

Even though data quality projects have been around for a
number of years in companies, the quality of information
remains patchy. Even worse, the tendency is for that quality
to be in decline.

---

7. Datawarehouse, Datamart. It can also be an Operational Data Store
(ODS). An ODS is a consolidation data repository, situated between the
Datawarehouse/Datamart systems and the production systems.

We shall see that in the absence of an MDM approach, attempts to rectify the quality defects do not bring sufficient gains. First, though, it is important to define more precisely the "data quality" concept. More often than not, experts in this discipline do not take into account the determining aspects of time management, context management, and version management that influence data content.

1.4.1. *Data quality*

The quality of a piece of data can be measured by its meaning and its value.

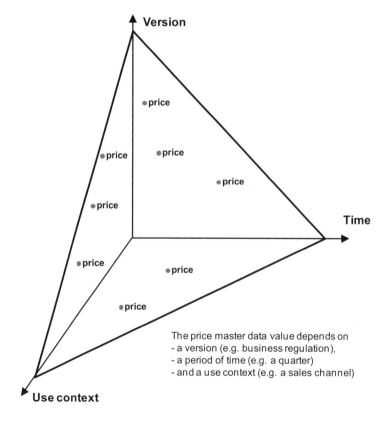

Figure 1.3. *"Price" master data with version, context and time axes*

The English phrase applied to the MDM field expresses this quite well: "one version of the truth". But this simple explanation is not always entirely achieved, for two main reasons:

– the first is the result of data duplication in multiple systems. In the event of conflict between different values, from one database to another, a quality problem appears. How do we find the correct value?

– the second reason, less obvious, takes into account the new forces that are in play in IT systems. These forces appear along three lines: time management, context management and version management. Data must be positioned in this three-dimensional space, as it is otherwise impossible to govern its value (Figure 1.3).

1.4.1.1. *Time management*

A single piece of data can have a different value over time, be it in the past or in the future. For example, an organization can update data for a future date in order to prepare a regulation change. This time constraint is rarely taken into account sufficiently in existing systems, even though it is needed more and more. This requirement, which certain industries are already aware of, especially insurance companies under regulation pressure, is becoming more and more generalized. It is the corollary of the increase in the expectation of process traceability. Certain pieces of data, particularly sensitive to the time factor, are accompanied by periods of validity, enabling the process to acquire the correct value depending on the execution date.

Taking this into account is not always easy, especially when it concerns date validation management on links between data. For instance, an organization describes the relationship between a *product* and a *factory* for a given period of time, and then switches *factory* for another period.

At the time of execution of a supply chain process, depending on the execution date, the *factory* employed is different.

1.4.1.2. *Context management*

Companies work in networks at the international level or use multiple distribution channels. This ecosystem gives rise to a number of different management contexts, also called use contexts. From then on, an IT system cannot limit itself to working in a fixed context at the time of its design, in the context of the company that is its owner. It must adapt to the variations brought about by each of the different use contexts.

For example, the commercial conditions of a loan are personalized depending on whether it is proposed by a given distributor, sales channel or even a country, etc. These usecontexts change the way in which data is managed. A single piece of data can have a different value depending on its use context. For international companies, multi-language management is an already well-established case of contextualization. The value of the "product name" data is different for each country, even though it is in fact the same piece of data.

1.4.1.3. *Version management*

The value of each data is relative to a version. It can be a technical version (for instance a working version), or a business version (such as a regulation or, for example, a version of a chart of accounts). A version is created in a more cunning way than a simple copy and paste of the data. Indeed, a traceability link between the original version and the new one is established in order to compare and merge together data from different versions.

1.4.2. *The quality of data models*

Data quality is not simply concerned with the value of the data. If the data models themselves are not to a high standard then it is impossible to improve the quality of the data. Indeed, only a data model can give the meaning of data and their validation rules, without ambiguity and across the whole of the Information System.

Even the classic example of unduplicating of addresses is not immune to this: how is it possible to determine whether an *email* address is private, professional or temporary without taking into account its meaning? An *email* address located in a *marketing* database might also correspond to a personal address. The same piece of data is also stored in a customer orders database but, this time, corresponds to business address. The two addresses respond to different semantics; the data model must express these characteristics. The first is used in marketing operations and communicated to third parties, following customer confirmation. The second is used exclusively for sales and after-sales. One can therefore not be favored over the other. There are numerous examples to illustrate this, exposed by the same semantic faults: ambiguity surrounding the definition of the Client concept, loss of a sense of the Revenue concept, or of the Site concept (area, place), etc.

Furthermore, the meaning of a piece of data is likely to depend on definitions relative to other data. For instance, "the *Product* has to be linked to two *Manufacturing Units* in at least one *Factory*". This rule of data referential integrity is expressed in the model through the association between *Product*, *Manufacturing Unit* and *Factory* business objects.

When a company faces a situation where its data assets are spread out, it is not uncommon, for example, that the concept of a factory exists in multiple heterogenous databases. How is it then possible to guarantee that a product to factory association is correctly situated? Is there more than one meaning to the factory concept? Which data model should be used as a reference? Worse still, if the link between product and factory is handled at the time of process integration between the two databases, it is highly likely that the referential integrity constraints would be hidden in the EAI/ESB software, without proper documentation. Due to the fact that there are multiple associations between data and that companies do not properly master the links between databases located within their silos, it is understandable that the general quality of data is in freefall.

The data *squat* is noxious

In a number of systems, quality defects are such that the same piece of data can have different meaning depending on how it is used. IT experts call this a data *squat*; not knowing how or no longer daring to improve the existing data model, they employ a part of the existing model and give it a semantic of a different kind, with coding enabling a distinction to be made between data, giving an idea of its origin, and any hidden meaning. For example, a piece of data relating to a contract can be *squatted* so that it suddenly matches a type of insurance guarantee.

This type of madness is not unusual. A number of IT systems hide this toxic mechanism. With time, it renders the semantics of the data model useless; only a proper reconstruction of a semantic model can enable order to be restored in these systems.

Consequently, in order to improve the quality of data, it is imperative to have a rich data model at your disposal which takes into account all the links between the data and independent of artificial boundaries stemming from functional and technical silos. This is a semantic model, meaningful to business users as well as to IT experts.

Data quality improves once a company produces a semantic data model, before any action is taken to clean up the data. In other words, the use of data quality tools based on poor data models with a low-level of knowledge about associations between data, is not a satisfactory solution.

The structural problems of data quality are ever present: ambiguity concerning the meaning of data, errors during the exchange of data between silos and with third parties, different values for the same piece of data duplicated in several databases, inconsistent data validation rules from one system to another, etc.

1.4.3. *The level of maturity of data quality*

Today, the quality of data is handled vis-a-vis its data value only, which corresponds to the first level of maturity, one that can be qualified as "basic quality". This level is not concerned with the structure of existing databases. It is about sticking cleansing tools on to what is already in place, to attempt to correct the quality defects that the silos continue to make. This is a tactical approach, compensating for a data duplication situation.

This approach does not take into account the new forces that are in play in IT systems through "time management", "context" and "versioning" (see section 1.4.1). This level alone is insufficient to improve the sustainability of data quality because processes continue to update databases of mediocre quality.

The next maturity level entails putting an MDM system in place in front of the silos in order to create, in one location, the true version of reference and master data. This level attempts to get there without worrying about semantic modeling. MDM revolves here around a database that has a similar structure to the physical data models already in place. Even though this MDM system is not the one we recommend, it still adds to the quality of the data. It takes into account time, context and version management. At this stage, the maturity level is qualified as "extended quality". It is important to pay attention to this approach, because the capacity of MDM to evolve is generally not sufficient: without rich and stable data modeling, the company runs the risk of creating MDM systems through silos.

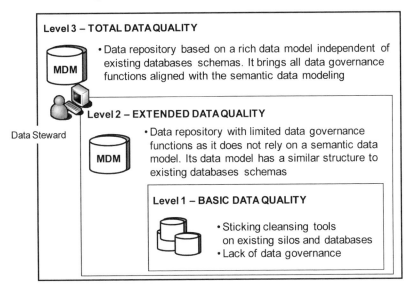

Figure 1.4. *The level of maturity of data quality*

Finally, the highest level of maturity is based on MDM taking advantage of a semantic data model. This rich data model is independent of the physical schemas of the databases; it expresses all the data meanings, with their relationships and their validation rules. Any intrusion into silos is still limited as the MDM system can be the object of an asynchronous technical integration with other databases (see Chapter 12). This rich data model takes full advantage of time, context and version management.

It is essential to deal with variants of the same data model, depending on its use contexts. For instance, the data cardinality that link two business objects are handled as master data, which allows different values depending on who is using the data. We call this level of data "total quality". It is necessary to employ a Model-driven MDM system so that the solution is directly aligned on the semantic model.

1.5. Different types of data repositories

Companies did not wait for the appearance of MDM to worry about the management of their reference and master data repositories. These data repositories have always existed. However, the manner in which they have been treated has been very variable: spreadsheets, direct IT access to database tables, tools used under the responsibility of IT, business software tools which are heterogenous depending on business departments, etc. Among these solutions, it is important to distinguish the three that can be classified as software packages and which are currently used in companies: Customer Data Integration (CDI), Product Information Management (PIM) or Product Life Management (PLM), and a repository for organization structures based on the LDAP (Light Directory Access Protocol) standard.

Before explaining the differences between these data repositories and an MDM system, it is important to first take into account a technical notion that are unfamiliar to the management or business world: the difference between *transactional* repositories and *semantic* repositories.

1.5.1. *Technical classification*

We will see in this section that a transactional repository is based on a classical database, whereas a semantic repository uses a rich data model.

1.5.1.1. *Transactional repositories*

A transactional repository is based on a transactional data model, i.e. limited to a simple description of data, without taking into account validation rules, time, context and version management, which we have already described. Most of the time, a relational style model is involved, as already well established. This model needs to be completed by other descriptions which enhance the knowledge of the data, in particular, validation rules. Because the additions are not integrated into the model, issues arise in terms of understanding by business users and IT maintenance. In fact, the additions are too often expressed in technical terms and hard-coded in software.

The weak expression levels of the data model do not favor the formalization of knowledge but allow good performance at a technical level. This repository qualifies as transactional since it is capable of dealing with big interactions without its response times worsening. Several thousand transactions can be executed in a short space of time, without the repository being a problem. Relational database technology supplies the technical aspects to handle a large volume of transactions. However, the rigidity of the repository means that software developments to each modification of the data model have to be made. The high value administration functions that are added, such as time, context and version management, are costly and not easy to deliver via this traditional software development. The consequence of this approach is to recreate silos, since creation of each new data repository is the same as creating a new database.

This repository is not the focus of this book. It is a repository based on a traditional data model which requires heavy software developments which are too much of a burden for the responsiveness and transparency needs of MDM.

1.5.1.2. *Semantic data repositories*

A semantic repository is richer than a transactional repository. The semantic model surpasses the classic relational model; it welcomes all the knowledge of the data, especially validation rules and behavioral variations depending on the use contexts of the data model. The semantic model enables a greater business user input in the knowledge specification.

To put a semantic model in place, you need an MDM tool capable of handling it in order to automatically obtain the data repository and all its data governance functions: input and data consultation screens, version management, context management, audit trails, access rights management, etc. It is no longer necessary to develop specific software to put the data repository in place.

The wealth of the semantic model makes the IT optimization of performance harder to ensure than with a classic relational data model. On the other hand, an MDM system does not have as many optimization needs as transactional data, for the following reasons:

– the volume/quantity of reference and master data are less important than for transactional data. On average, they represent 20% of a company's data;

– MDM users are the ones concerned with reference and master data governance. There are far fewer of them than there are of usual IT system users;

– access to an MDM system in real time is not systematic. In most cases, the repository flows into production databases. These databases then follow classic optimization procedures used in a relational oriented approach.

Finally, from a technical point of view, a semantic repository forms an abstraction layer above the classic systems of database management, such as DB2, Oracle, SQL-Server, etc.

Consequently, the power and reliability of these databases are always used and taken advantage of by MDM[8].

1.5.1.3. *Model-driven data repositories*

An MDM system must be based on a semantic model. It must be capable of taking into account any rich data model, whatever the data domain: product configuration, organization and third party description, financial classification, charts of accounts, technical parameters, etc. This MDM system can also qualify as a Model-driven MDM system, because the data repository is largely governed by the rich data model.

Without taking into account the semantic repository, MDM remains a similar solution to a hard-coded software development based on a rigid and frozen database. The use of a database schema from the transactional world (a relational DDL) in order to deal with the data governance needs of the reference and master data is not relevant. MDM needs agility and a Model-driven approach based on a rich database (XML) schema.

Throughout this book, except when clearly mentioned, the term MDM will mean Model-driven MDM.

---

8. From a technical point of view, MDM acts in this case like a DAL (*Data Access Layer*) or, more precisely, ORM (*Object Relational Mapping*).

1.5.2. *Customer Data Integration (CDI)*

It is not uncommon for a company's customer knowledge to be spread out over a number of databases located in a number of systems, such as in a Customer Relationship Management (CRM) database, an Internet database, a billing system or a marketing database, etc.

To synchronize these databases, companies complete their technical integration layer with a storage solution in the form of a transactional hub, called Customer Data Integration (CDI).

The image of a hub illustrates well how CDI operates: all the modifications to customer data are sent to the hub which is responsible for verifying their validity, keeping data in its database and notifying other systems of the update, often in real time. The higher and more frequent the quantity of exchanged customer data between systems is, the more a CDI looks like a classic database, i.e. a transactional repository.

Its transactional foundation does not enable CDI to manage a rich data model. Therefore, a large part of the data validation rules and referential integrity constraints are hard-coded in bespoke software outside the CDI. In other words, the rigidity of the data models leads to a deficiency in data governance functions. CDI is not driven by the data model; it is not Model-driven. Consequently, the data governance functions are frozen at the start and cannot be easily adapted to the evolutions of the data model. It is a rigid approach, of a heavily integrated software package kind.

Even though the use of the semantic data model to automatically generate the data governance functions is appealing, Model-driven system cannot always replace CDI. The highly transactional aspect, especially in the case of CDI for B2B third parties (individuals, citizens) does not allow this all of the time. In that case, it is best to couple a transactional hub with MDM.

Indeed, there are a number of reference and master data that define customers. For example, classifications, hierarchies, incorporation of customers within geographical sectors or socio-economic categories, customer risk levels, etc. All this data must be governed even before transactions are executed in the hub. On the other hand, certain transactions carried out at the CDI level could cause rejection of information that is in one's best interest to submit to the MDM system in order to benefit from its data governance functions. For instance, if the CDI detects that a client is not connected to a mandatory classification, then it can send a part of the file to the MDM system so that a data steward can complete it.

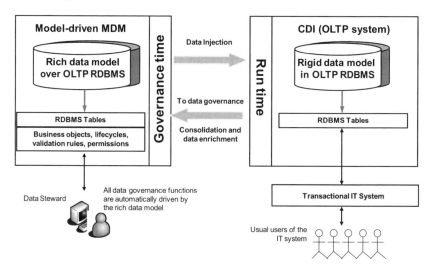

Figure 1.5. *Collaboration between CDI and MDM*

A collaboration therefore appears between CDI and MDM (see Figure 1.5):

– the first acts on the transactional aspect, i.e. in run time;

– the second acts on data governance, i.e. in governance time.

1.5.3. *Product Information Management (PIM) and Product Life Management (PLM)*

For a long time, companies have used software to manage the design process of their products with solutions called Product Life Management (PLM)[9] systems.

They also use software for the configuration of products to marketing standards, or for manufacturing and sales, using Product Information Management (PIM) solutions.

PLM and PIM are based on flexible data models enabling the complex configuration of products, but not yet semantic in order to directly express within the models all the data validation rules. PLM and PIM bring with them certain constraints:

– software developments, sometimes heavy and often rigid (hard-coded), are necessary in order to implement the data validation rules that cannot be stated in these models;

– the flexibility of the data model is dedicated to product management. It is not possible to use PLM and PIM for data other than products;

– when the description of a product needs to be connected with other business objects, for example factories or employees, a disconnect in the data repositories appears, due to the fact that PLM and PIM can only harbor product information. In the end, PLM and PIM recreate silos on

---

9. For more information on PLM, see [DEB 04].

product repositories, generating integration difficulties with the rest of the Information System.

PLM is different in some ways to PIM. In particular, PLM has important functions for collaborative work. These functions enable concerned parties in R&D to work collectively on successive versions of a product as it is being designed. Furthermore, PLM integrates itself with CAD/CAM systems through data interfaces on technical nomenclatures and digitally-controlled machine tools. Once a product is put forward by R&D, it is then copied into the PIM repository to make it accessible to marketing systems, and to manufacturing and sales. With PIM, product configuration operations occur, but on the basis of pre-established parameters at the time of product design by R&D, i.e. on exiting PLM.

The close relations between PIM and other data repositories (supplier, customer, factory, marketing, etc.) make the use of MDM inevitable. Thus, MDM must replace PIM. It is important to have a semantic data model for product configuration in order to build an MDM system that can be integrated with other data repositories, without any unnecessary breakdowns[10].

With PLM, the choice of its replacement by an MDM system is a more delicate affair. Indeed, an MDM system needs interfaces enabling it to interact with subsystems used by an R&D department, such as CAD/CAM, etc. This effort is justified if a company notices that the integration of PLM with the data repositories in production, be it a PIM or an MDM system, is problematic. In an economic environment where the design and manufacturing lifecycles are ever increasing, a breakdown between a R&D and the other marketing, manufacturing and sales teams could have a

---

10. This approach is also possible when using software packages (see Chapter 3 later in this book).

negative effect. In that case, MDM must replace PLM, as long as it is able to integrate the subsystems of R&D and that the workgroup functions, i.e. its workflow data approval, are adapted.

1.5.4. *Lightweight Directory Access Protocol (LDAP)*

Among the most common data repositories, the one that is concerned with the description of an organization is very important. It holds the description of the geographical, organizational structures as well as the people involved. It can also contain other descriptions linked to a number of a company's assets.

Under the effects of functional and technical silos, IT looks to rationalize the "directory" aspect of organization description. This deals, in particular, with the unification of user identifier and password management used to authorize access. An LDAP IT standard is adapted to this type of repository. In this way, most software packages, operating systems and desktop solutions are compatible with this standard, which allows directory access to be rationalized.

Over time, this directory has taken a wider turn, integrating partner descriptions, other information about contact details (email, telephone, etc.) and also administrative assets (conference room, projector, etc.) in order to supply resource reservation tools. Going from a functional use, the limitations of LDAP becomes obvious. These limitations are linked to the absence of business governance functions. Only IT experts can manage LDAP data, especially as they become more and more complex.

The associations between business objects, for instance, between the description of a manager and their administrative assets (offices, projectors, computers, books, etc.) are difficult to handle adequately. In the end, facing the absence of governance functions, an LDAP data repository is centered on its initial competency domain, i.e. the management of user identifiers and passwords.

A collaboration between an MDM system and LDAP is an interesting possibility. The MDM system is upstream of an LDAP in order to govern all the data linked to an organization. Only a part of this data is then exported to an LDAP repository so that the applications, software packages and desktop subsystems can access them in the usual manner.

Having come to the end of this chapter, we are in possession of a good analysis of data repository positioning within a company.

In the next chapter, we study the strategic impact of an MDM system in supporting enterprise governance and the transformation of Information Systems.

Chapter 2

Strategic Aspects

In an environment where IT is a problem for companies, it is important to understand how its restructuring entails regaining control of data, starting with reference and master data repositories. The MDM approach meets these demands. We will elaborate on this response, from a strategic angle, through what it brings to corporate governance and through the transformation it brings to information systems.

2.1. Corporate governance

Why bother restructuring an IT system? Is the official report of an IT burden on business enough to shake up the entire company to make in-depth changes to the existing systems? In most cases, this realization is not enough. Other factors need to be taken into account if IT is to be changed.

The first factor is of technical origin. A company's IT systems might be obsolete. If the platform for execution is no longer maintained, software must be migrated to a lasting solution. This situation can lead a company to invest in a technical migration of its software, with no added value to the business.

The second factor concerns the business directly: any regulatory constraints can weigh on an IT system. In a tense economic context, these constraints are more numerous, ever changing, less predictable and more strategic for a company. It could be said that business regulations have forced Information Systems and IT systems against the wall.

2.1.1. *Forced against the wall by regulations*

Directors worry about regulations because of their obligatory nature. They do not have a choice and have to respect them all: Sarbanes Oxley, Basel 2, MIF, Solvency II and others relative to fiscal archiving or to sustainable development, the food industry and pharmaceuticals. Regulations are the rules of the economic game, as imposed by a country's legislature. Not respecting them, within imposed time limits, will lead to penalties for a company, and could even put its capacity to act on the markets in jeopardy. This aspect greatly affects a company's shareholders and their representatives, i.e. the board of directors. This is a true matter of corporate governance.

Today, the valuation of companies operates more and more through rating systems linked to regulations. A good rate and shares climb; a bad rate and shares plummet. The link between rating systems and IT systems is immediate. These regulations require a high level of operation traceability. A company must be able, just as for merchandise in the food industry, to track the information flow precisely, keeping a record of any data that contributed to the calculation of financial and social accounts. When rating agencies value a company, they must have tangible elements at hand that guarantee the truth surrounding the accounts and the respect of regulations.

The more opaque an IT system is, the less information the rating agency has. The existence of software under the sole control of technical experts does not make it possible to judge alignment with regulatory requirements.

The opposite is also true: the more an IT system increases its transparency by using business repositories, especially master data and business rules repositories, the more a company has a determining advantage to act on markets in a way that conforms to law. A process repository (a.k.a. a BPM) is less of a determining factor because legislation is not interested in the way in which a company is organized. Business regulations are more concerned with the respect of data, and rules traceability and auditability.

2.1.1.1. *Compliance and governance risks*

Faced with the pressure of regulations, a new corporate management domain has appeared with *Governance, Risks management and Compliance* (GRC), which aims to manage the risks and guarantee successful sustainable development for a company, while at the same time limiting errors and fraud. Software vendors have dived into this field proposing business solutions for risk management. Sadly, most of these business software suffer when it comes to integrating them with the rest of an IT system, especially with the synchronization of data repositories with those already in place in a company. It is necessary to study the introduction of this type of solution with care because there is a danger of creating a new application silo, based on a risk management scope, not in line with operational systems.

On the contrary, risk management must be integrated with production systems. In order to do this, it is not enough to place a new software package in the IT system landscape, even if it were specialized in risk management. As long as IT systems are not based on a unified, transparent and reliable management of data repositories, risk management and alignment with regulations will remain approximate.

2.1.1.2. *Electronic business regulations*

Legislators are becoming aware that regulations must be translated in a reliable and transparent way within company IT tools, without which it is impossible to follow through with their application. Sadly, most of the time, this IT translation is based on desktop tools, such as spreadsheets, which are too elementary.

Security and access management, data entry and update traceability and version control are non-existent or handled in a unreliable and cumbersome manner. In order to straighten out this problem, business regulations are increasingly presented in a new format, meaning one directly useable by IT.

Legislators no longer only produce a rule book but also reference and master data models and business rules: some must feed a company's data repository and others a system of business rules management[1].

When these new kinds of laws are introduced to companies, the organizations that already have experience in data repository management (MDM) and rules repository management (Business Rules Management System (BRMS)) have a considerable competitive edge. They are able, more rapidly than others, to adapt their way of operating to the imposed regulations and demonstrate their capacity to ensure the traceability of their data and business rules.

Companies must anticipate this change of direction towards business repositories. They should also seek financial help from the public purse, for instance by tax optimization of IT investments that support the work of real risk management.

---

1. See in particular the *"Governance, Risk Management and Compliance Roundtable"* community: http://www.grcroundtable.org/

2.1.2. *The new scorecard*

The importance of risk management means that a company must have indicators for the piloting of the transparency levels of its IT system. To do this, it must consider the intangible asset shares made up by its reference and master data and business rules. These shares must be delivered all the way to board level.

Boards of directors, representing a company's shareholders, must be able to verify that their IT systems revolve around the valuation of intangible assets based on reference and master data, and business rules. This is the most secure way of guaranteeing that the traceability is enforced as required by business regulations.

Therefore, MDM is situated at the highest level of strategy, at the disposal of corporate governance. It revitalizes scorecard solutions by adding information coming from business repositories, that Business Intelligence systems neither have the ability nor the means to produce[2]. New KPIs are therefore at their disposal, and enable decision makers to better follow the data and rules assets, in particular any evolutions outside of the norm:

– intangible asset share stability: each month a share differential is calculated. It enables the progression of the take-on of the repositories by data domains to be judged (clients, third parties, products, financial structures, real estate assets, etc.);

– number of defects of the master data asset, by defect type: poor quality, lack of reliability, valuation defect, etc.;

---

2. Business Intelligence systems run on consolidated data and statistics, whereas an MDM system has data which is detailed, operational and synchronized with production systems.

– analysis of the impact of data defects on the execution of processes by impact type: process failure, subsequent entry with delayed processing, malfunctioning with partners, with clients, etc.;

– number and type of disparities vis-à-vis regulations: delay taking into account a new version of a business regulation, inability to take into account one part of a regulation, putting a regulation into place outside of the intangible assets (for instance directly managed in Excel spreadsheets), etc.;

– frequency of queries and updates by intangible assets and organizational unit. Monthly analysis of these frequencies in order to be able to judge the activity of the organization regarding its master data and its business rules,

– amount of effort dedicated to training personnel by intangible asset;

– financial valuation of these shares[3]; etc.

Before reaching such a mastery of an IT system by its business repositories (data and rules), it is necessary to transform what is already in place. This transformation must not put in jeopardy the current activity of a company. It must be carried out in a progressive manner, without imposing a big-bang effect that would be impossible to negotiate. We are now going to show how this is possible.

2.2. The transformation stages of an IT system

Faced with cumbersome and out of date IT systems, stemming from several decades of bespoke developments as well as use of software packages, a company often no longer has the means to replace its IT in one go. An organization

---

3. It is then necessary to have rules to evaluate assets, in the form of an accounting approach of a quantitative, qualitative and financial nature.

can be incapable of brutally cutting itself off from its existing IT because it is involved in all decision making and operational tasks. The improvement of the situation is made in stages, but voluntarily stopping investments that intensify the addition of extra layers of software on top of what already exists, the control of which can no longer be ensured.

An IT department must slow down the addition of software if it is not able, at the same time, to take away what is no longer reliably working. Businesses users must demand a more transparent IT, which means taking the reference and master data, business rules and processes out of existing hard-coded software. The progressive restructuring of IT systems must be based on this re-appropriation of intangible assets strategy. The first stage is MDM, the foundation of the whole transformation, followed by a business rules repository (BRMS) and processes (BPM).

2.2.1. *First stage: the data repository*

The MDM approach is deployed with no impact on what already exists, i.e. without modifying the data repositories which are already in place in any historical databases.

The MDM situates its data repository, a kind of reference and master data warehouse, in front of existing functional and technical silos. A data synchronization mechanism between the MDM and these silos allows the replication of updates from the MDM to the already existing databases in the silos. In order to achieve this, IT specialists must master technical integration solutions[4] that enable this synchronization.

---

4. Type EAI/ESB/ETL.

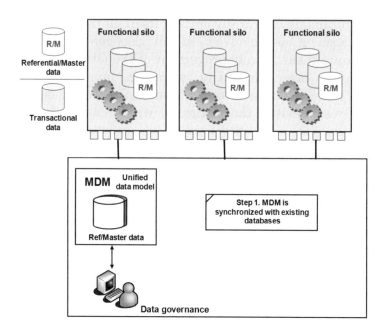

Figure 2.1. *First step: the data repository*

For instance, a large regional bank holds a legacy banking IT platform, with repositories to configure its products and services that bring together thousands of reference and master data values. Certain values in this data depend on the specifics or business variants within the regional banking branches. The bank personalizes its products and services, depending on the region. In the existing IT system, the reference and master data is trapped in files and heterogenous databases (VSAM, DB2, Oracle and other configuration files) but also in software packages. The user interfaces of this data administration are heterogenous, not very ergonomic and not sufficiently secure to make them available to business users. The functional teams express their banking product configuration needs in the form of textual specifications. These are retaken manually by IT staff who become responsible for setting the parameters of the banking products, without wanting to or having the skills. In the context of constant product evolution, the bank and its regional branches perceive this IT solution as a burden. How is it possible to improve the situation without questioning the operation of the existing banking platform, the overhaul of which, in one go, is impossible when you take into account the enormity of the task?

This bank is confronted with a strategic problem that links directly to MDM. Indeed, the approaches of BPM, SOA, Business Intelligence or others are bound to fail because they require taking charge of the reference and master data up front. The processes (BPM), the exposed services (SOA) and the Business Intelligence systems remain mediocre in quality if the data they are handling is not reliable and only governed by IT.

With MDM, this bank is building a unified data repository for its reference and master data; it has a homogenous user interface under the responsibility of the business users who administer them. Without intrusion vis-a-vis the existing files and databases, this new data repository is synchronized with the one already in place, via integration solutions. The heterogenous consultation and reference/master data update screens, in the existing databases, are neutralized to the benefit of the governance functions brought by the MDM. The transactional systems of the banking legacy platform are not impacted by this new data repository architecture. These systems continue to use reference and master data in the historical databases, without knowing that they are now updated from the MDM system.

In some situations, a study on the impact of the existing user transactions might be necessary, for instance if a transaction is able to directly update a master data element. In this case, it is necessary to ensure that the MDM system is also synchronized with these transactions. This type of situation exists but is limited. Indeed, the reference and master data, by definition, is validated before use by transactional systems. There are more consumers of data than producers, at least in 80% of cases.

In the end, this bank, without modifying its existing IT platform, will be able to reduce the opacity of its reference and master data management by putting a data repository and adequate governance functions into the hands of its business users. This type of project lasts for more than just a few weeks.

First of all, the bank must start a semantic modeling of its data. This modeling provides a business view of data, i.e. independent of the physical data structures of existing databases. This model is used by the MDM system and allows an automatic generation of administrative functions: consultation screens and data updates, version management, audit trail, etc. The access rights on governance functions are clarified in order to decide what the data repository management responsibilities should be. For instance, if the bank so wishes, it could be possible to delegate the management of certain product configurations to regional agencies. The aim of this management is not to directly update the production environment of the banking platform. Consequently, a validation process (undertaken by the bank's headquarters) of configurations proposed by the regions is put in place. The MDM system then supports the approval process of data updates (workflow).

2.2.2. Second stage: the business rules repository is added to the data repository

The second stage of the transformation is concerned with business rules. We will not describe here the use of business rules for reference and master data validation in an MDM. This is useful when rules become complex and can no longer only be registered in the data models.

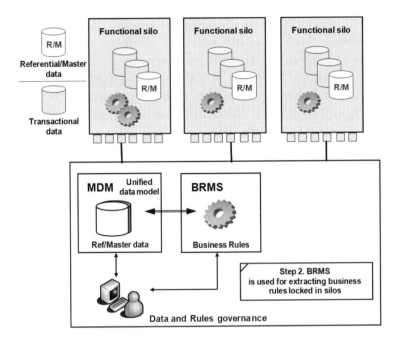

Figure 2.2. *Second step: the rule repository*

More broadly, we will discuss here the extraction of business rules locked in the silos. As is the case for reference and master data, these rules are scatttered in hard-coded software, in languages which are heterogenous and incomprehensible from a business perspective. The business auditability of this software is impossible. Similarly, administration functions such as version management of rules is no longer available, or too technical, and in any case only available to IT managers. In a similar fashion to MDM, a company can start a Business Rules Management System (BRMS) approach in order to get certain business logics out of the existing hard-coded software and have them translated into a rules language before being placed in a rules repository.

In the first phase of the transformation, it is possible to act without modifying the existing software in depth. It is enough to neutralize certain components of the software in order to replace them by a call to the rules management system, the behavior of which remains identical to that of the original software. Gradually, a company realizes its software assets through the rules repository. Even though the functional behavior of the system does not change, the business regains the knowledge via the rules management. The administration functions brought by the rules repository, in particular version and context management, enable a revitalization of the IT system. Business users can write different rules depending on the use contexts of the software, for example whether a subsidiary, a regional agency, the HQ, a partner, or a regulation version, etc. Without this rules management, only IT specialists are able to act on the system in order to personalize its behavior, depending on whether it is a subsidiary or HQ, by directly modifying the software. With the rules repository, the software assets can be assessed by a business rules inventory, under the responsibility of business teams.

The rules repository is even more strategic when it is coupled with a data repository. This coupling enables the use of business rules across the whole IT system, in a secure manner, since the BRMS benefits from a unique and reliable access point to reference and master data. Therefore, the rules repository exploits the data repository during the authoring of rules and during their utilization:

– during the authoring of a rule, its author must often choose between data values in the repositories to describe its behavior. For example, for the rule "If the Type of Product is equal to 'EXT-PARC-01'", the value of the type of product must be selected in the product catalogue repository, in the correct version. This repository is managed by the MDM system. Consequently, the business user or IT staff member who authors this rule also has access to the MDM system;

– during the execution of a rule, it processes transactional data as well as reference and master data. The former is communicated to the rule by the business process that sets it off. The latter is directly retrieved in the MDM repository.

At the end of this second stage of the IS transformation, the company has a new IT system backbone at its disposal which embraces the first two intangible assets of reference/master data and rules. All that remains now is to take into account the last asset, that of business processes.

2.2.3. *Third stage: adding the business processes repository*

Acting on what is already in place, in a non-intrusive manner, is key but can also turn out to be insufficient. A company is constantly evolving and its software must be in line with the business undertaken. After having succeeded in regaining control of what is already in place, via business rules and reference/master data repositories, it is time to overhaul the IT system.

New developments benefit from the reference/master data and business rules that have already been capitalized.

As this overhaul progresses, new rules emerge to enrich the repository. The reference and master data, if they have been correctly modeled during earlier stages, stay as they are. Making the most of this overhaul, a company can review its business processes taking care that they do not code them into hard-coded software. At this stage, Business Process Management (already well known by corporations) enters into play. The processes, administered in a dedicated repository, are based on the rules provided by the BRMS and the reference/master data provided by the MDM. The circle is thus closed: the processes, the business rules, and the reference/master data are under control. A new IT system is born: an open IT system for business, more open to evolution, and more sustainable.

The reader must remember a crucial point with regard to the IS transformation that we have just described, concerning the use of the process repository.

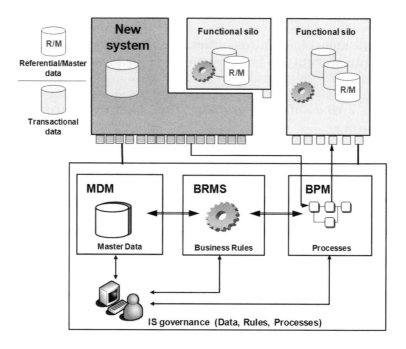

Figure 2.3. *Third step: the business process repository*

The process repository intervenes in the last stage of the transformation, once the data and the rules are properly handled within the data and rules repositories. Too often, companies adopt a contradictory approach that aims, first of all, to deploy a business process repository. Due to the fact that they use rules and data, it is easy to predict that the processes will remain of a mediocre quality until this data and these rules are better managed in the repositories.

The coupling of MDM, BRMS and BPM follows a protocol that cannot be altered, without risking failure. It is first necessary to ensure semantic modeling of the data, and then handle the business rules to at last renovate the processes. This is not about creating a tunnel effect that forces a company to wait for final completion of data modeling work before beginning the rollout of rules and processes. We will see, in the section of this book dedicated to the method, that it is possible to model data iteratively, by subsets, which also permits the progressive establishment of rules and processes.

This novel approach to the IT system, based on the three repositories, gives birth to the concept of a Sustainable IT Architecture. This concept goes against the legacy IT system, too often trapped in opaque IT incapable of incorporating the repositories. We will now elaborate on how this Sustainable IT Architecture is truly of strategic value to the company.

2.3. Sustainable IT Architecture

The term "Sustainable IT Architecture" was used for the first time in 2009 in *Sustainable IT Architecture –a progressive overhaul of the IS with SOA* [BON 09], which deals with the progressive transformation of an IT system, from a technical point of view, basing itself on MDM, BRMS and Service Oriented Architecture (SOA).

Figure 2.4. *Agility Chain Management System (ACMS)*

MDM was already important then and was integrating itself into the novel concept of the agility chain or Agility Chain Management System (ACMS). [BON 09] highlighted, from an IT engineering perspective, that the agility level of a piece of software is equal to the weakest link in the chain consisting of its reference/master data (MDM), its business rules (BRMS) and its processes (BPM). Indeed, as the processes are based on business rules and these are based on reference and master data, there is no point in being agile about the processes and the rules, if, at the same time, the reference and master data is neglected.

2.3.1. *The new management control*

The Agility Chain Management System (ACMS) guides IT in the right direction for the transformation of systems, putting in place an MDM system, BRMS followed by BPM, in that order. This order is logical as soon as the agility chain is understood and taken on board. This is also an order, however, which is the complete opposite to that chosen to most of the transformation attempts selected by companies. It is easier to start a process renewal because it does not require a very big modeling effort. Of course, the processes are modeled, but they are treated as objects localized above the existing IT. These processes claim to orchestrate operations which for the most part would already be available in the existing IT system. They are therefore applied as a logical complementary layer, with no impact on the heart of the system in place, which nonetheless imposes rigidity and reliability problems. This approach is like putting a plaster on a broken bone, with no chance of treating either the pain or the handicap. Worse still, in delaying the required steps for too long, the fracture mends in a way that sets the handicap in a way which is all but irreversible, ensuring a long legacy.

The sustainability of an IT system can be measured via the materialization of its IS assets, following the order defined by the ACMS.

When a company has a bank of processes, which have come from a BPM approach, this will have no value if at the same time, there is no bank of business rules.

This statement can destabilize many managers convinced of the benefits of taking only a BPM approach. Such managers only look at it from the point of view of a quality that is meant to improve the IT system by normalizing, documenting and automating company processes. In reality, they are only maintaining non quality by creating an additional layer, and leaving the situation unchanged. IT still suffers as the BPM task lists continue to use business rules and reference/master data scattered throughout the IT system, poorly documented, of poor quality and insufficiently transparent for business.

Sustainable IT Architecture requires that control management of IT extends to control management of the Information System, with an analytical accounting that is based on ACMS, i.e. a bank of reference/master data, business rules and processes. This accounting must evaluate these stocks of data from a quantitative, qualitative and financial point of view. This is achievable, and an entire book should be dedicated to it. Companies begin to perceive the strategic interest of such a viewpoint in favor of the transformation of IS and IT systems. There are multiple advantages to analytical accounting and it helps IS transformation.

Even though, at first, the intangible asset stocks are low, a comparison of these stocks at different points in time allows us to judge whether or not the transformation is headed in the right direction. These objectives can be fixed by managers, forcing businesses and IT to collaborate, on identified domains of the IT system, in order to progressively build asset banks. New software developments are written for this control of management and must justify their contribution to the assets. Software is no longer seen as a cost but rather as a contributor to intangible assets. Managers, at the highest level within a company, must have performance indicators specified by both the business and IT department together, which present the strategic follow up indicators of analytical accounting brought about by the ACMS.

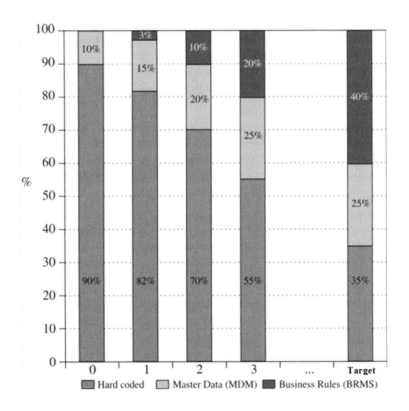

Figure 2.5. *Example of intangible asset evolution (source: SMABTP)*

Figure 2.5 illustrates the evolution of intangible assets, over a number of years of IT system transformation, within the insurance company SMABTP [BON 09].

2.3.2. *Maintaining knowledge and the strategic break*

Intangible assets, properly described and well-accounted for, enable a company to benefit from a considerable lever in the maintenance of the knowledge domain, for the practice of business, as well as for IT practitioners. Knowing an IT system via its intangible assets allows us to learn about it much more rapidly and reliably:

– business users no longer get caught up in existing IT that is often the only way to gain access to certain business knowledge. Instead, they have a direct access to intangible asset stocks. Maintaining knowledge, in particular within complex and evolving organizations that characterize modern companies, cannot survive the trap set out by fixed and stratified hard-coded software, nor informal (textual) documentation, rarely up to date and non executable. Intangible asset stocks are expressed at the same time in formal terms, understandable by business users, governable with no IT knowledge, but also directly executable by the tools of the MDM, BRMS and BPM;

– IT practitioners focus on the technical quality of software i.e. the infrastructure that must use the tools of the MDM system, BRMS and BPM. They return to their original business, that of IT engineering. They have a methodological role and accompany business users in their assets modeling, and managing them over a given time period. They no longer have to assume business knowledge, which is impoverished anyway, in compensation for the one that no longer completely exists on the business users' side.

With the right management of IS assets (master data, business rules and processes), the IS and IT situation changes in a radical manner. For companies that do not understand this quickly enough, this is the same as using analog data storage systems when their competitors are using digital systems. In this context, the competitiveness of a company, one step behind its IT system, is seriously called into question. A sustainable IT architecture creates a strategic breakdown. This is not some future breakdown. The methods and techniques exist to act in this way, progressively, without a big-bang effect. Our previous book, *"Sustainable IT Architecture"* [BON 09], has already shown certain ways to do this, particularly in the hands of IT specialists. Among these procedures, it is necessary to understand that the MDM approach is the launching pad of the Agility Chain Management System (ACMS), and therefore of the new control management of IT systems that we wish companies to have.

At this point in our thinking, it is time to concern ourselves with business software packages. Are the MDM approach and the transformation of the IS that we describe here compatible with software packages?

Chapter 3

Taking Software Packages into Account

The MDM approach has the same advantages and is based on the same implementation procedures as when a company has business software packages such as ERP, CRM, Supply Chain, etc. Whether software packages are already in place, or whether new ones are acquired to revitalize existing IT systems, it is important not to be locked in these software. The reversibility or easy replacement of software packages must be favored by taking their IS assets into account. These are formed by their reference/master data, rules and process repositories. To achieve this, the software vendors must work towards taking into account this reversibility; it has less to do with the technical than the strategic impact.

3.1. The dead end of locked repositories

A software package exploits a "locked repository" when its data, rules and processes administration functions are dedicated to its own scope. In the reference and master data domain this means that the software package has an MDM solution that is limited only to its data. We identify this

MDM system by the expression "locked MDM" which differs from "enterprise MDM". This latter is in agreement with the unified approach of repositories across the whole of the information system which is presented in this book.

At first glance, a software package which has a locked MDM system at its disposal could be an attractive option. A company could judge that it will save by not putting an MDM system in place, as it seems to already be acquired with the software package. Unfortunately, as soon as it is necessary to leave the boundaries of the software package, it is difficult to maintain a unified approach to repository management. It is necessary to put in place other MDM solutions, outside the software package, that lead to an architecture by silos of repositories. It is rare that a software package covers the totality of needs even though its reference and master data must be shared across the whole company, by all IT systems. On the other hand, a software package must retrieve reference and master data stemming from other IT systems, outside its own administrative scope. In the end, accepting an MDM system locked in to the scope of a software package, is the same as maintaining or reinforcing the silo effect that nevertheless needs to be corrected.

It is important to give preference to software packages that favor IT neutrality in terms of the management of reference and master data, i.e. that accept integration with an MDM approach across the whole of a company, uniquely capable of guaranteeing the following benefits[1]:

– the quality of reference and master data is reinforced since the MDM silo effect is counteracted. Only one solution for the management of reference and master data is deployed across the whole of the company; those that exist in software packages are neutralized. This neutralization does not

1. See the criteria for choosing businessware in section 3.2.

concern databases, but only their administration functions. Just as for existing systems, an MDM system is synchronized with software packages' databases, without any intrusion into the processing provided;

– there is a better reversibility of software packages. As soon as the reference and master data, followed by the business rules and the processes, are situated in independent and neutral repositories, the software package is reduced to a technical engine. A company is then more autonomous at the time of a change in strategy for its computerization. It can change software packages without losing its reference/master data, business rules and process assets;

– the ability of a company to open up towards its partners is increased if, for example, some data needs to be revealed beyond the boundaries of the company. It can be done using an enterprise MDM system, without linking to software packages which can remain in the background, invisible to its partners.

Once this approach has been acquired for the reference and master data, a company can adopt it for business rules (BRMS) and processes (BPM) in order to obtain the same reversibility and unification gains.

3.2. Criteria for choosing software packages

In the boxed "Business case study" below, an industrial firm is able to integrate its software packages with an enterprise MDM system because the software vendors gave their reference and master data models as well as the programming interfaces of their repositories.

Business case study

Acting in the high-tech semi-conductor domain, an industrial firm implements new software packages for customer management and manufacturing operations. These software packages have their own product configuration repositories and, without calling them into question (impossible given that they are at the heart of the software packages in use), an enterprise MDM system is employed to manage the configuration of these products autonomously, on a neutral IT platform.

This MDM system covers the full life cycle of the data of each product, from customer specification to production and sales by the company. Synchronization of the MDM is therefore made with several software packages, each responsible for a part of the life cycle (PLM, ERP, supply chain) and a part of the products' attributes.

These data synchronization procedures enable the MDM updates to be replicated in the software packages. Rather than use software package administration screens, business users access the unified MDM administration functions. The company reduces its reliance on software packages as its intangible asset based on the configuration of products is not linked to the software packages. The asset is situated in the enterprise MDM repository, a kind of data warehouse of reference and master data, the life expectancy of which is greater than that of the software packages.

When the company interacts with partners or absorbs other firms, it shares its repository without having to provide access to its software packages. An absorbed firm can supply its own software packages and specific developments with the help of the MDM system, without being forced to move its organization into the parent company's software packages.

These are two essential conditions for reconciliation of the MDM approach with software packages. Last but not least, when a locked MDM system exists in a software package, it is necessary to neutralize its administration functions.

3.2.1. *Availability of the data model*

The data model must be available and documented. It must distinguish between reference/master data and transactional data, which is not easy when the model is built on the basis of an overlapping of two different data types, with no distinction. This availability of the data model represents a real change in the commercialization policy for most software vendors.

The data model must be communicated in a standard notation such as UML or another DSL. One version presents the model in a comprehensible manner for business users and another, more technical, is aimed at IT practitioners. The first constitutes the semantic model that expresses the meaning of data, their associations and validation rules. The second is the logical data model that provides the coding rules of the data and the information necessary for its technical integration. A translation of the logical model to a physical data structure is also necessary, for example in an XML form. In conclusion, it is best to have all of the description of the highest level data (semantic) right through to the technical implementation (XML) via the logical level.

By benefiting from the modeling already available in the software packages, on the condition that these are of an adequate level, a company can avoid starting its own modeling from scratch and can control its semantic model so that it does not unnecessarily differ from those imposed by the software packages used.

3.2.2. *Repository updates*

A software package must provide programming interfaces to update and query its reference/master data repository. These services are used to implement the synchronization of data between the enterprise MDM system and the software package.

A detailed study of these services is necessary in order to analyze how the software package deals with evolved data administration functions. In particular, the data version management functions and the data entry by uses contexts (multi-language, multi-regions, multi-channels, etc.) are not always available within the software package. In this case, two approaches are possible:

   – invent a mechanism in order to add, in the software package data model, the information necessary to the version and context management. If the data model is not extensive, then the involvement of the software vendor's R&D team is necessary to achieve this;

   – abandoning administration functions related to version and context management. This abandonment would mean the end of a real enterprise MDM system because modern organizations need these functions. It is one of the important conditions to raise the agility of information systems and increase their transparency and auditability (see Chapter 1).

3.2.3. *Neutralization of a locked MDM*

When a locked MDM is present in a software package, two approaches are possible. It is necessary either to:

   – neutralize its administration functions to favor those brought by the enterprise MDM system. This implies that the software package does not overlap with the management of transactional data and reference/master data on the same screens. Indeed, by neutralizing the data repository user interface, it is important that this does not cut the software package off from some transactional management screens. If the software package is not properly clear on this point, it is necessary to carry out an analysis of all the screens and judge the overlap levels between these two data types; or

– admit that the software package remains "master" on a subset of reference and master data. Therefore, the operational teams can continue to create certain domains of reference and master data (example: Articles) in the ERP, but this data is consolidated in the enterprise MDM system, undergoes a validation/enrichment life cycle on a much larger data model, and then is re-synchronized with the software package.

Other administration functions of a locked MDM system must be studied in order to decide on any overrides. For example, the audit functions of data consultation can be preserved. Similarly, default procedures of repository safeguard are generally maintained.

3.3. Impact for software vendors

What remains in the scope of software packages once the reference and master data, their business rules and processes are externalized into the MDM system, the BRMS and the BPM, respectively?

Software packages change their nature; they must be capable of interacting with the three repositories. A software package's benefits are then found in the integration between processes, rules and reference/master data. It retains the responsibility for transactional data management which, by definition, is not found under the control of the MDM system. This new kind of software package reduces its business ascendancy and raises its technical responsibility (see Figure 3.1).

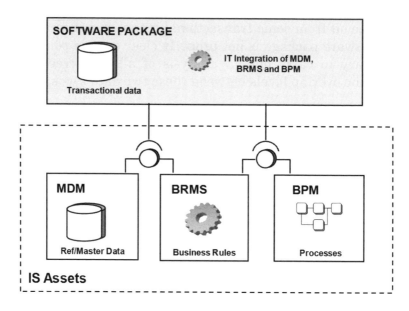

Figure 3.1. *The structure of a new software package*

The software vendors must rethink their value proposition by marketing intangible asset stocks. That is to say, a reference and master data stock, in the form of data models and an off-the-shelf implementation in an enterprise MDM solution. Similarly, they would be better off proposing stocks of business rules and processes immediately operational in the rules and process repositories tools.

The innovative software vendors are orientated towards the commercialization of intangible IS assets rather than the sale of integrated solutions that no longer meet IT system transparency needs.

Software vendors do not always perceive this necessary evolution of their offers in a positive manner. Indeed, when the transformation strategy is carried out under the terms we are explaining, then the software package imprint on the IT system is reduced, in favor of a new independence achieved with the help of repositories.

Consequently, market pressure is needed so that software vendors take into account the new requirements that we have described. This is already the case in the business process management field: it is usual that software packages are capable of situating business processes in BPM solutions, outside of their scope.

This must also be the case with MDM, and the BRMS.

3.4. MDM is also a software package

The objective of independence for software packages has been identified by companies, especially after the sometimes painful experiences of a first wave of computerization, not only for ERP, CRM but also PIM and CDI[2].

The reconquering of the independence approach vis-à-vis software packages, thanks to the repository-based approach, knows no alternative. It would not be reasonable, however, for a company to launch into the development of a specific MDM software solution. The technological and business barriers are too strong, especially when delivering administration functions such as version management, enrichment of data by context, traceability functions, user interfaces which are secure and sufficiently friendly for business users, etc.

A company must acquire, on the market, an MDM software solution which offers all the administration

---

2. See Chapter 1 for the positioning of PIM and CDI.

functions necessary for business users. The independence sought vis-à-vis software packages could be hindered here. Indeed, an MDM system is a software package. It specializes in reference and master data governance functions; it does not impose a specific data model; its value resides in the complex ability that it produces in the IT system to manage reference and master data assets. However, it still remains a software package.

Technical note: XML and XML schema

XML and XML schema standards are well known in the IT field and business users do not need to worry about them. Nonetheless, knowing that they exist is fundamental in order to demand that the technical solutions take them into consideration. It is an important precaution that favors the reversibility of IT solutions.

XML and XML schema have been established by an international organization (World Wide Web Consortium (W3C)) that also deals with Internet standards. They came into existence circa 2000 and have established themselves in IT. These standards enable the representation of rich data structures that integrate all the business knowledge which is established in semantic modeling.

An MDM software package, in due form, must be compatible with these standards. All the knowledge of reference and master data must be absorbed in the standard description in an XML schema (with the necessary technical extensions, for example in order to manage associations between business objects) so that there are no other descriptions that are trapped in a proprietary format.

As with other software packages, the degree of independence in relation to an MDM system can be questioned. Is it possible to change an MDM system over time, if necessary?

This reversibility allows a company to be the trustee of its reference and master data models. A company must make the effort to formalize the knowledge of its data, even if it is based on pre-built models, to avoid starting from scratch. Then, the models must be translated into an IT standard format that enables the MDM software package to be changed without losing data or models.

This IT standard is a must; it must be XML for the data and XML schema for the physical representation of the data models.

If these two conditions are not respected, then companies could encounter problems, in time, if they should change their MDM tools; otherwise, the knowledge of data and its implementation in XML and XML schema standards guarantee a full reversibility.

Chapter 4

Return on Investment

The MDM approach, used across the whole of an IT system, requires a new budget to support the reorganization and manage changes, launch and support data modeling work, install software solutions, and to connect the data repository to IT systems in order to synchronize the databases. Nonetheless, this investment can be carried out in a progressive manner, without turning the existing systems upside down. This is made possible by reconciling the Enterprise Architecture approach to data, associated with a gradual implementation of each data repository. Work on each repository provides a return on investment, at the same time as correcting existing faults but also giving the company new opportunities in which to maneuver, via improved quality and reliability of data, mastering of operational risks, transformation of the IT system.

4.1. Financial gain from improved data quality

The first potential source of financial benefits that must be studied is that arising from the lack of quality of reference and master data. Companies are faced with this low quality in their everyday activities, for example when sending out erroneous financial reports or sending incorrect data flows to partners. This is also the case when customers benefit from incorrect discounts due to errors in the products and services configurations customized through new sales channels, such as the Internet.

For example, for several hours, one financial company offered an abnormally low credit rate on its website following a master data input error. An increase in subscriptions took place, probably as a result of viral marketing, the net result of which was detrimental to the company. Similar examples are endless, as they occur daily in organizations.

A number of studies exist to alert companies to financial losses induced by problems in lack of data quality, for example *The Data Warehousing Institute* (TDWI) indicates in its *Data Quality and Bottom Line* report that: "The Data Warehousing Institute estimates that data quality problems cost U.S. businesses more than $600 billion a year" [ECK 01].

Unfortunately, the financial valuation of this quality does not often exist. It most often becomes part of a mountain of hidden costs, the existence of which is not revealed in any management control. Yet these costs do exist:

– what is the cost of the loss of new business potential with a partner because they no longer have confidence in the quality of information from the company? This business partner, as it extends purchases to new types of products, no longer accepts the order consolidation problems due to data coding issues between products which are needlessly heterogenous, such as order categories, payment types, type of product returns management, etc. As the company extends its sales strategy to services, these data coding discrepancies are amplified because the underlying IT system is structured in silos, with heterogenous databases for products and services, without unified code management;

— what is the price of not respecting a business regulation due to financial statements with non auditable reference and master data? This data may be locked and dispersed in databases that are unable to restore a full and unified data history that can be used by business users and auditors of business regulations;

— what is the price of a poorly managed personnel rotation due to heterogenous descriptions of posts and skills with different data coding depending on production lines, with no reason other than the IT silos that trap the data in heterogenous technical structures?

Nothing prevents taking these malfunctions into financial consideration in a new management control that would go beyond the single accounting view. It is then necessary to integrate the analytical keys giving way to a measure of the quality, in financial terms. In the absence of such a management control reform, it is often necessary to rely on a more statistical approach, based on samples, i.e. such as those that we have just given. This exercise will considerably reveal hidden costs that the MDM approach can correct.

4.2. The financial gain of data reliability

Financial losses due to the reliability of information are less studied than those of non quality, even though they are significant. Data which is of poor quality almost immediately penalizes anyone exposed to it. A reliability defect does not always result in an immediate problem for the process that uses it. This problem will resurface later, which renders execution of any necessary corrections more complex. The longer the delay, the more significant the risk of a large-scale spread of the problem. It is important to weigh the difference between reliability and data quality:

– when data is not of a good quality, its value is quite simply wrong. It must not be used by the business processes;

– when data presents a certain level of reliability, its value can be used, on condition that the processes are able to tolerate it.

Let us take the simple example of the email address of a client. This address has a different degree of reliability depending on whether it has been automatically retrieved from the internet during a publicity campaign, bought with a marketing file, given by a teleoperator, or directly validated by the client himself on a secure website.

What attitude should be adopted when faced with these different degrees of address reliability? Should the least reliable address be substituted with the most reliable one? (This is the same as allocating a reliability scale depending on the way in which the address was obtained). Should all the variations be saved and the business processes themselves be allowed to decide upon the correct address depending on their needs?

These approaches, and perhaps others similar to them, are all valid and depend on the case in question. Not taking into consideration this reality which influences a number of data could turn out to be dangerous: data has a level of reliability that depends in particular on its source. Our example of the email address nicely illustrates the degrees of reliability, but is not very representative of the risk incurred in cases of poor data use.

Let us take a second example, more acute: a company must manage a formal classification of its financial operations and assets in compliance with a business regulation, in the spirit of Basel 2. This allocation cannot always be done in an automated manner; human intervention is often necessary. Several players are likely to intervene to decide on an allocation, sometimes with a level of certainty that is not absolute. The choice of asset classes is important as audit controls are likely to highlight errors and reduce the company's rating. Furthermore, certain financial statement consolidations are based on these classifications of assets. Before implementing an MDM approach, this company used tools which were not strong enough to deal with the classification (in part based on an Excel-type desktop management), which users were not able to sufficiently coordinate to produce reliable classifications. Faced with large financial flows which needed to be classified, managers would make the users proceed to classifications, even if the level of knowledge remained fairly approximate on certain types of flows. Unfortunately, users were not yet able to indicate the degree of reliability of their classifications. They were under the control of managers who needed to liquidate the flow assets that needed to be classified, at all cost, including a lack of reliability as they did not feel the immediate consequences. The mediocrity of this system went as far as stopping users from correcting themselves because, due to the fact that they knew nothing of the reliability of the classifications, they did not dare modify them, even when errors that needed to be dealt with were obvious. How, then, do we correct information if we don't know who is responsible for it nor its degree of reliability?

Thanks to an MDM system for financial flows, this company secured the classification management of its flows. A census was done, for each user, in order to determine degrees of reliability for each type of financial flow. This level of reliability is then associated with all flow classifications.

If a user, for a previously identified type of flow, has a level of reliability inferior to the information on classification which is already at hand, then the MDM system forbids the modification. On the other hand, if a user identifies a classification error that s/he wishes to correct, s/he can do so if s/he holds a degree of reliability superior to the classification already in existence. This MDM system integrates the notion of information reliability in order to control update authorizations. It is a powerful device that enables this banking company to be better aligned with business regulations. The gaps in the requirements of this regulation could induce strategic problems, going as far as a declassification of the bank in the rating systems.

A better management of data reliability is an important vector in the valuation of an MDM system. Taking this into account is too often neglected in favor of an approach which is only directed towards data quality.

4.3. The financial gain of mastering operational risks

Atypical behaviors in an organization, i.e. those not closely related to an expected function or considered normal, must be detected as soon as possible.

This is of strategic interest: it means highlighting abnormal situations that could lead to a company taking unacceptable risks. These risks have a financial value that we are looking to regain, or more precisely not to lose, by putting in place a supervision solution applied to the whole Information System and its underlying IT systems. We will see that the MDM approach considerably contributes to this.

4.3.1. *An all too often inefficient control system*

The supervision of an Information System is fairly simple to describe. It is an execution of a set of business rules that enable the surveillance of operational tasks carried out by a company. These rules must be specified by business users;

they correlate data in order to detect certain atypical behaviors.

For example, it could be highlighting situations such as:

– the address of a third party which is modified more than five times during a quarter;

– a classification key of financial flows created and then deleted in a period of less than two hours;

– an employee allocated more than three positions in less than six months;

– a product which changes manufacturing units more than twice in a week.

IT specialists must rapidly implement these rules, as easily as possible, in order to be able to integrate new ones without surplus software costs. How can they do this when the tracked data is dispersed in databases within functional and technical silos where they are out of reach?

Let us reconsider one of the above examples, that of the modification of a third party address that we wish to keep an eye on. How can IT know the number of times this address has been modified in a period of time, when it is stored in several databases, in the CRM, in the billing system, in an Internet database? To make matters more complicated, it is highly likely that the databases are not all capable of restoring a full and unified data history of their updates which can easily be used. The IT practitioner does not have a choice: s/he suggests a bespoke software development in order to add surveillance programs for distributed data. They might perhaps put in place a database of the address history on which the supervision business rules will be applied? This is a sort of atrophied MDM, lacking administration functions for business users, under the sole control of IT. It takes time and leads to a locked solution.

Such a control system is as opaque as the information system that it is meant to monitor!

This is an additional sign of the difficulty IT has in aligning itself with businesses. Each new supervision business rule requirement leads to a new bespoke software development. The greater the surveillance requirements are, thanks to the experience that business users have acquired, the more the business rules correspond to a great deal of data. This data has a greater probability of being stored in different databases, which increases the difficulties for IT specialists.

This control system, as strategic as it might be for the company, becomes obsolete, maybe even nipped in the bud, if those in positions of responsibility know how to anticipate the brakes that we describe here, and judge that it is better not to send teams into this dead end.

However, the need for surveillance remains. It is more and more necessary with the increasing complexity of organizations. We will see below that MDM answers this requirement.

4.3.2. *MDM for the control of operational risks*

Since reference and master data are available in an MDM system, in a reliable manner, it is from this that any supervision business rules must be activated. From then on, the marginal cost of the implementation of any new rules is practically nothing. As the data is available in a reliable location, IT practitioners no longer need to develop specific software to gain access to the data processed by the rules.

Certain rules also take advantage of transactional data that are not in an MDM system, unless they are in the definition of duplicated data between systems (see Chapter

1). For these non-duplicated transactional data, it is easily accessed as they have a unique storing location.

Once this surveillance strategy of the Information System and its underlying IT systems is understood, what is the return on investment of an MDM? What budgetary promises are directors and board of directors ready to agree to in order to better manage operational risks?

MDM becomes a kind of insurance against risks. Since IT is present in all the decision processes and operational tasks, the surveillance system, on condition that it has correct and reliable data in an MDM system, offers a considerable risk detection capacity in real time, and a very rapid adaptation in face of changes.

4.4. The financial gain of IS transformation

We have already seen how a company must act to transform its IT, worn out by time and dealing with complexities too great for it to handle (see Chapter 2). The use of data repositories (MDM), of rules (BRMS) and processes (BPM) is the key to this transformation. We will now study the financial evaluation of these repositories. To justify the necessary investment to the transformation, a new asset must emerge, the valuation of which is greater than that already in place.

But, how do we estimate the value of IT and, while we're at it, the whole Information System? This question is not a new one and has never found a satisfactory response. We need one, however, as without it all idea of a transformation is stopped dead in its tracks. The answer does exist: it is found in the genes of the transformation approach that we are describing. To understand it, we must first look at the strange overlap, favored by time, between an Information System and its underlying IT systems.

4.4.1. *The overlap of an Information System and IT*

First of all, it is necessary to note that the value of IT is unknown. It is perceived as a cost center. The management school INSEAD notes this several times in its study on the evaluation of IT assets: "Firms have managed their core software assets not as an asset for value creation but as an expense item to be minimized. This has to change." Further, "56% of all CIOs and CFOs feel that the financial value of the organization's core software assets were not or poorly assessed as compared to other corporate assets such as brands and intellectual property" [DUT 07].

At the same time, if IT systems disappeared, in an imaginary scenario, it is plausible that a company would not recover from it. All modern organizations undergo and maintain an intimate overlap between IT and their business processes. From there, we can consider, surprisingly, that IT has an infinite value, since without it a company cannot survive.

This reasoning holds no credibility with decision makers. Management control has no place for assets with an infinite value! In reality, it is not IT which is important but the Information System that is executed through it. If the Information System stops, then the company is in danger. IT, from this point of view, is just a tool. This tool should be reversible, almost a technical commodity, without value, just as an electrical network brings energy. But we are very far from this at present and this may never come to fruition.

This also fully affects companies that have strategies based on software packages, because they undergo cumbersome and costly IT customization projects. The software package often becomes a piece that is unique and non reversible, like traditional specific and bespoke developments.

This lack of reversibility is indicative of a dangerous coupling between Information Systems and their underlying IT systems. In our imaginary scenario of an IT system which collapses entirely, the Information System would also be at a standstill, and it would be impossible to fix software within reasonable time spans and costs. This overlap is fatal for a company. It renders IT heavy, unavoidable and intolerable.

To change this, it is imperative to clarify the financial valuation of the Information System and its underlying IT. Once the IS assets are better understood, it is easier to situate them in a sustainable technical infrastructure, isolated from the rest of IT. We will now see how.

4.4.2. *Financial valuation of an Information System*

The objective of transforming an Information System means putting in place procedures that favor its independence vis-à-vis its underlying IT system. To achieve this objective, more than half of software developments, carried out in a bespoke manner by hard coding, should be deleted in favor of a formal management of reference and master data, business rules and processes in MDM, BRMS, and BPM repositories, respectively.

This approach is not always properly appreciated by certain IT systems integrator firms who prefer to have classic development projects, mobilizing software developers. Rather than bet on offshore to reduce costs, companies must take MDM, BRMS and BPM repositories into consideration in order to streamline IT development and reduce risks, costs and time spans. In any case, these repositories are the only way to propel the assets of an Information System into the hands of business users.

Hard-coded software with complementary repositories are less weighty but are more important. They ensure the link between data, rules and processes repositories in order to enable processes to interact with business rules, and for the latter to use reference and master data and other data that resides in transactional databases. This IT infrastructure is specialized in the implementation of an IT engine that fully benefits from repositories. This engine is a technical commodity that could, if the company perfectly mastered it, become reversible. Therefore:

– the Information System is freed from unnecessary constraints that tie it to a part of its underlying IT systems that disappear in favor of data, rules and processes repositories;

– this freedom from constraint is seen in reference and master data, business rules and processes stocks, and is also embodied in administration functions that enable business users to govern these stocks.

On the basis of this transformation, the answer to the question concerning the valuation of the Information System is at hand:

– the value of IT is calculated based on its capacity to interact with MDM, BRMS and BPM repositories. IT must first demonstrate its capacity to interact with an MDM system. Then it must demonstrate its ability to join the BRMS with MDM. In the ultimate phase, it demonstrates that it masters the interaction of the BPM and the BRMS. The order of this chain of interactions is a determining factor. It must be dealt with in this order as it corresponds to the logic of regaining control of the whole system: first the data, then the rules and finally the processes. This transformation requires time; to avoid an unnecessary tunnel effect it is necessary to establish a plan of action that would enable an MDM system, BRMS and BPM to be deployed in successive slices;

– the value of the Information System is measured via its assets, finally exposed and measurable, via reference and master data, business rules and processes. This stock must be recorded and followed in a new management control system.

This financial spotlight has many consequences for businesses and IT managers. The former face the valuation of their Information System assets. A decrease in valuation can reveal a lack of control of the reference/master data, business rules and (more rarely) process knowledge. IT managers are evaluated on their ability to put in place a new IT agreement with business users.

This agreement holds the MDM system, BRMS and BPM repositories in the software development and maintenance contract that defines the relationship between business users and the IT department.

4.4.3. *The MDM as a springboard for transformation of IS*

The whole transformation strategy is based on mastering the repositories. The return on investment of the MDM system can then be measured by the expected value of the new targeted system. It is necessary that business users remain vigilant in the way that the MDM system is perceived by IT. If it is reduced to being seen as an improvement solution to the quality of reference and master data, then its implementation risks being atrophied in relation to the more global transformation objective. MDM is first and foremost a modeling approach; the quality of data is only the corollary of modeling efforts.

This modeling must not be specific to the reference and master data. Let us take the example of a product catalog. The business object Product is described by more than one master data, from its configuration. But it also exists via business processes, i.e. the transactions which support the activity of the company, like, for example, order entry processes and replenishment processes within the company. In particular, stock information is not included in the master data definition (see Chapter 1); rather, it is transactional data.

Therefore, during the modeling of reference and master data, certain patterns of this modeling will be valid for the reference and master data as well as for transactional data. These are business objects and their business states[1]. Consequently, the foundation of the reference and master data modeling is, in reality, nothing more than the enterprise data architecture, including both reference/master data and transactional data. This data expresses all the information that the company handles, beyond the sole scope of master data.

If this aspect is not properly understood, then the company runs the risk of modeling reference and master data that cannot be used as a launching pad for the re-appropriation of transactional data. This re-appropriation comes, after the implementation of the MDM system, as the progressive transformation of the IT system gets under way.

At this point in time, these modifications require the setting up of transactional data models. If other business objects, with other business states, are used, this provokes a distortion between the reference/master and transactional data.

The financial valuation of the MDM approach also goes through the return on investment of the modeling effort. If

---

1. These states are necessary in order to make the validation rules of the master data more reliable. For more detail on this, see Chapters 8 and 9 dedicated to semantic modeling.

this modeling is not reusable at the time of the modeling of transactional data then a financial loss is recorded (that of the restarting from the beginning of transactional data).

Moreover, if distortions between the reference/master data and the transactional data appear, then discrepancies between business objects risk rendering the alignment of the MDM with the business rules management system unnecessarily complex. Indeed, the rules must exploit the same business object, whether they be reference/master or transactional data.

For example, a rule that manipulates reference/master and transactional data of a "product" business object at the same time must get all this data from the same business object. There would be no sense in having a "product" business object as master data, and one or more others for transactional data. This would leave the door open for inconsistencies in the management of data.

4.5. Summary of the return on investment of MDM

Having arrived at the end of this chapter, what do we have at hand to justify, from a financial point of view, an investment in MDM? Unfortunately, it is impossible to provide figures outside of the context of a real company. However, we do have the criteria for financial analysis, and they are shown in Table 4.1, following the order in which we have described them in this chapter.

Example of issues that the MDM can fix	Financial consequences before correction by the MDM system
Data quality (section 4.1)	
Erroneous value of a discount rate (abnormally low)	Subscriptions that affects profitability
Poor consolidation of orders from a partner due to hetereogenous coding of products	Loss of potential business with partners
Inability to provide traceability of data used for the setting up of financial statements, auditable by regulations	Decrease in the company's rating by regulation auditors
Reliability of data (section 4.2)	
Ambiguity in the reliability of the email address of a third party (is it the email for marketing campaigns or for commercial relations?)	Unnecessary disruption for third parties when using the commercial email address for marketing purposes
Classification of financial operations by assets depending on the requirements of a business regulation. This classification is carried out without the business users being able to say the degree of reliability with which these decisions are taken	Mediocre asset classification as the business users cannot correct the problematic classifications due to the non traceability of decisions: a business user cannot modify a classification if he is unaware of the degree of reliability of the person who is responsible for it. Decrease in the company rating by regulatory auditors
Mastering operational risks (section 4.3)	
Inability to detect that the address of a third party is modified more than five times in one quarter	Increase of a bonus fraud during the change of address
Inability to detect that a financial classification key is created and then deleted in a period of less than two hours	Embezzlement in financial operations

Late detection of the fact that an employee has been allocated more than three positions in less than six months	Personnel demotivation, abnormal turnover, increase in work related accidents
Inability to detect that a product changes manufacturing units more than twice in one week	Anomaly in the optimization process of the manufacturing of products that financially penalizes factories
Transformation of SI (section 4.4)	
Scattering of master data, business rules, and processes within hard-coded and opaque software	Dangerous overlap between the Information System and its underlying IT systems explaining the brakes on the latter. The IT budget dedicated to maintenance is extortionate: any business change requires complex and costly work for IT staff. Management control is incapable of taking into account Information System assets (reference and master data, business rules and processes), which is the same as a defect taking into account value. IT masks this value by trapping it in opaque software
The improvement of data quality is handled only by working on its value without being preoccupied with data models	Data quality does not progress; it has a tendency to be degraded with the growing complexity of organizations and systems. The economic performance of the company is penalized by these quality problems
The lack of a tool enabling business users to govern reference and master data	Financial loss due to unnecessary communication with IT to ensure the needs of business, for the initialization and modification of reference and master data, is taken into account. Increase in the poor quality of data. Inability to take into account the reliability of data. The company is weakened by its data, which diminishes its economic performance

Table 4.1. *Criteria for financial analysis of an MDM system for business practices*

PART TWO

MDM from a Business Perspective

Chapter 5

MDM Maturity Levels and Model-driven MDM

Three levels are used to evaluate the maturity of an MDM system: virtual, static and semantic.

The lowest level uses only virtual MDM; the highest level requires the practice of semantic MDM. Between the two, static MDM presents certain risks in relation to data quality because it may create inconsistencies in the data repository. It is important to have a clear understanding of the differences between these three levels so as not to create false expectations from users, as only semantic MDM interests business users. We will also see that a more detailed technical analysis of MDM leads to the concept of Model-driven MDM.

5.1. Virtual MDM

Virtual MDM answers a problem which IT faces when information is linked across several databases. Take the example of a product which is associated with a list of factories. If the information is stored in the same database the links are managed automatically. The retrieval of factories linked to a product presents no issues.

However, if the products are stored in a separate database to that of the factories, for example each in a different functional silo, a software infrastructure is required to manage the associations.

When a large number of data elements are duplicated across many databases, with multiple links, this infrastructure becomes complex. Sometimes the same data object can have different identifiers depending on the database in which it is stored. In the absence of software offering a unified vision of the links between the objects used in the different databases, the data integrity rules are difficult to manage in a reliable manner. For example, when we modify the attributes of a factory, it is necessary to find all the attached products so as to check that these modifications are compliant with existing products configurations. If the products are spread across several databases, IT specialists must build bespoke programs to gather a consolidated and unified view of all products for the factory. In the same way, queries which require links to objects stored on different databases can be costly to put in place; they require bespoke developments which negatively affect system performance and can be costly (because of development and maintenance) and negatively affect response times and integrity.

To overcome these problems, IT practitioners can put in place a virtual MDM system. This MDM system only manages the identifier of the objects, their links and their locations in the databases; it does not contain descriptions of the data objects; this is why the term "virtual" is used. The body of the data is not stored on this MDM system. It is also called a broker, mostly when it supplies data mapping between the identifiers of the same business object. For example, a customer has an identifier equal to IdValue#1 in a legacy database in DB2/MVS and another value IdValue#2 in an Oracle/Unix internet database. The virtual MDM system manages a mapping table between the two identifiers (IdValue#1, DB2/MVS and IdValue#2, Oracle/Unix) so as to unify, virtually, the scattered customer information, artificially, across two different databases.

Sometimes, virtual MDM expands the description of the objects using a header record which is frozen when the object is created. It is not possible to update this subsequently. For example, for the business object "Contract", it may be the date and place of adhesion to the contract which will not change in the future. These headers are used to optimize queries by utilizing the static data in the objects: if the header information suffices, it is not necessary to access databases spread across different silos.

Virtual MDM allows better control of the integrity rules which link objects across multiple systems. It constitutes a master database for the teams in charge of systems integrations[1].

It has been stated that this type of MDM system does not include knowledge of the data elements that make up the objects.

Consequently, the functions of business administration do not exist. It is not possible to put forward a way of managing versions, using a unified user interface for data entry, modifications, and queries, managing a full and unified audit trail on data use, etc. The value of this type of MDM, for business users, is limited. The opaqueness in the administration of reference and master data remains the same.

---

1. In the EAI/ESB.

5.2. Static MDM

Static MDM is most widely used in companies today. It can also be the most dangerous because it is not always enough to ensure full data integrity. It is not enough just to put in place MDM processes to automatically increase the quality of data. If the data repository relies on a model which does not adequately include data validation rules, it can lead to increased data quality issues. For example, in a financial data repository, if a business rule forbids the creation of more than three levels of financial classification, the MDM system must formally include this rule. If this rule becomes more complex, because the levels of classification change depending on the status of the financial operations, a more sophisticated data model, including validation rules depending on status is required.

In the absence of rich modeling, the MDM system only handles the static view of the data, which necessitates a hard-coding software development to implement data validation rules.

In this situation, the MDM system and its ad hoc heavy and hard-coded routines located outside the data model, becomes an additional application silo needing complex software maintenance. This MDM system becomes weighty and difficult to maintain.

A static MDM system, as opposed to a virtual MDM system, contains the reference and master data of business objects. It does not limit itself to managing the identifiers and associations between objects, nor a frozen header record at the moment of creation. This data model allows the storing and update of all reference and master data without restrictions. It is a true data warehouse. This MDM system allows updates, which means it must ensure a complete control of the data validation process. Business rules are required to check the integrity of data, both in pre-condition and post-condition during data updates. For example, an interest rate is valid for the MDM system only if the value corresponds to a maximum calculated in relation to certain parameters related to a period and a sales network. Under this rule, the period and the sales network are themselves master data hosted in the MDM system.

Data structures can be complex, involving data dependency links and associations between business objects. Consequently, validation rules must ensure the data integrity constraints even in complex data models.

In particular, data modifications must take into account the state of the business objects involved in the updates. For example the update of a product description can be dependent on its state: "to negotiate", "outdated", "archived", "activated", etc. Any modification may be disallowed if the product is not active. We will return to this idea later in the book. It is an important concept that concerns all the business objects in the system: product, employee, customer, partner, other third parties, statements of accounts, organization etc. These data objects hold different states which define their lifecycles. Depending on their lifecycles, the updates allowed are not always the same.

These constraints, relying on the business objects' states, are significant validation rules that the MDM system must take into account in a formal way. A static MDM system is unable to do this. It is not just a technical limitation but one of methodology; neither the data modeling nor the implementation takes into account the different states. The consequence of this is the implementation of hard-coded rules in software surrounding the MDM system. This failure to formally take into account business objects' states in the MDM system causes serious issues:

–   this type of MDM system is not seamless for business users. The MDM administration team is unaware of the specific hard-coded developments required for the management of the states; business users are unaware of the existence of these states. The business objects' states are buried in opaque software;

– this MDM system is unable to detect certain update errors due to the fact that it fails to take business objects' states into account for validation purposes at the moment of data updates. This gives rise to poor data quality, with serious risk of distributing that bad data to the heart of the systems using them.

These risks are not taken into account by the maturity level of the static MDM. It does not see business objects' states as master data itself. It is a weakness that can prove fatal. A static MDM is only valid if the system can ignore the states of the business objects. This can be acceptable for rare types of data which have simple structures and are outside the core of business objects, such as, for example, lookup tables for codes and labels.

IT specialists can be deceived by this form of MDM system. At the beginning of the process they may be convinced that static management of the data is suitable. However, at the time of user acceptance testing, and under pressure from their business users, they might be forced to add, in a way that is both rushed and insufficiently analyzed, data integrity rules and validation on the edge of the MDM system, i.e. by hard coding software developments outside the data repository. At that stage, it is too late to carry out a formal analysis of the states of the objects. In this kind of scenario the failure of the MDM system in the medium term is a risk: complex processing, added on the periphery of the data model, renders any real administration of the data by business users impossible.

Knowing the data also means understanding and mastering the data validation rules, and these often take into account the states of the business objects. If the state values are controlled only by IT specialists, in bespoke software which are inaccessible to the business itself, then the business administration of the data is sidelined. To counter this risk it is necessary to look to the next level of maturity: the semantic MDM system.

5.3. Semantic MDM

A semantic MDM system takes into account all the richness of the data, in particular the management of the business objects' states. The idea of semantic modeling has been looked at in previous chapters and will be looked at again when covering the procedures associated with methodology, in the last part of the book. This approach to modeling does not satisfy itself with just describing the data; it is also interested in the definition of validation rules and in the lifecycles of the objects through their states. Taking into account this dynamic aspect of the modeling is unavoidable to design and master all the data knowledge. This way of modeling is not easy to understand, either for business users or for IT practitioners. However, it is necessary to examine it in more depth in order to understand its importance in the MDM approach.

Why is taking into account the management of business objects' states complex but unavoidable? First, the states that are being described here are those which describe the behavior of the business objects as opposed to the states that describe the processes in the organization (data approval processes, workflows). At first sight, this distinction between the business level and the organization level is not obvious. Let us take an example to demonstrate the difference. The business object "Product" follows a lifecycle which can be described by a series of business states of the type: "opened", "suspended", "outdated", "archived", "to be negotiated". These states are linked with each other by transitions. For example, a product goes from "to be negotiated" to "opened" once the actors responsible for the negotiation have come to an agreement with the suppliers of the product. Whatever the organization puts in place to allow the actors to carry out the negotiation, the business object product must, at the beginning of the negotiation, have a state of "to be negotiated" and, at the end, have the state of "opened".

Between these two states, which can be described as business states because they are independent from the organization, other states of an organizational nature can appear. For example, the organization applied to a subsidiary requires that the actor in charge of the product negotiation obtain the validation of both the manager in the subsidiary and at head office (two organizational states), whereas, for head office, only one authorization is required (one organizational state only). For the same set of business objects' states, it is possible to have several organizational states which complement them according to requirements.

These states are included in the specification of the data validation rules. For example, the modification of the characteristics of a product is forbidden if its business state is not "opened". Semantic modeling requires a formal documentation of these states and validation rules. Taking these states into account lends invaluable support to the success of the MDM approach:

– an improved administration of data by business users;

– a greater reliability in the data repository;

– an efficient preparation for the integration of the MDM system with the rest of the system.

We will cover these points, in order, in the following sections.

5.3.1. *Improved administration by business users*

With a static MDM system, the states of the business objects and their effects on the data validation rules are not meaningful to business users. They are hidden in bespoke and hard-coded software. If a new validation rule linked to the business states arises it is necessary to plan for IT software development. With a semantic MDM system it is no longer necessary to resort to this type of development. The administration functions of this MDM system allow the management of the business objects' states as master data. The value of these states initialized and updated with the help of an administration function under the responsibility of business teams. In the same way, the addition of rules which allow or disallow the update of data (according to the states of the business object in which it is held) is handled by an administration function.

By avoiding the development of hard-coded software, a semantic MDM system is more in line with business requirements. As soon as data modeling includes the definition of the lifecycle of objects, a semantic MDM system takes them into account automatically. This is a considerable bonus in the business administration of data: it reduces the opacity that a static MDM system continues to harbor.

In having business objects' states at their disposal, teams can audit them, access the data modification rules that are dependent on the states, and check that there is no confusion between business states and organizational states[2].

5.3.2. *A greater reliability in the data repository*

By using the business states as master data, an MDM system can oversee their validation. In this case, a semantic

---

2. Business state = decision table (see Chapter 9). Organizational state = workflow (see Chapter 11).

MDM system knows the transition rules between business states and uses them to check their modification. For example, in a system where a business object "product" cannot move from state "expired" to state "opened", the MDM system is the guarantor of this rule and systematically prevents this update.

A semantic MDM, with the help of business states, ensures that updates do not corrupt the lifecycle of business objects. In other words, whatever the organization puts in place, the states of the objects are in line with the rules defined by the business. This separation of concerns between the business layer and the organizational layer is important. Organizations can evolve while the heart of the way in which business is carried out stays the same; it therefore becomes impossible to corrupt the core business even if errors appear at the level of the organizational processes.

In this way it is possible to manage organizational variants, without compromising the functioning of the heart of the MDM system. These variants can co-exist and kick in according to the organizational context faced (e.g. headquarter, subsidiary, country, channels etc.); they all rely on the same core business execution, in a secure and reliable way.

5.3.3. *Preparation for MDM integration with the rest of a system*

Data models have to take into account the requirements which go beyond those of reference and master data. They must:

– position the models in an enterprise data architecture common to that of transactional data;

– facilitate their integration with the rest of the Information System and its underlying IT systems.

We will now look at these two points.

5.3.3.1. *Enterprise Architecture*

Business objects and their lifecycles are not specific to MDM; they are the same as for transactional data. The coherence of the MDM system with the transactional data models is maintained by the re-use of a common foundation, which is based on the business objects and their lifecycles. We will see, in the section dedicated to method, that there exist two other common concepts between reference and transactional data: these are the grouping of business objects by "Data Category" and then at a higher level, by "Business object domains".

If the common foundation is successful, the modeling required for the overhaul of the transactional data will be based on that of the MDM system. The modeling of reference and master data, when it is achieved with the level of maturity of a semantic MDM system, is a springboard for the subsequent overhaul of IT systems.

5.3.3.2. *Integration of MDM with the rest of the system*

Data managed by an MDM system has to be synchronized with existing databases as long as these have not been redeveloped. This raises questions: is it necessary to update the silos databases with each MDM update? Should these updates be grouped together and, if so, following what criteria?

The states of business objects help to find the correct answer. Indeed, the synchronization of the data is carried out by taking advantage of the business objects' states. Rather than each update in the MDM system generating an update in the existing systems, several data updates can be grouped together and submitted when the business objects' states change.

These states must therefore be available in the MDM system, in a structured way. A semantic MDM system matches this requirement. Instead of the complex management of a large number of data synchronizations, it is more efficient to group them and rationalize them in relation to the management of the business objects' states: better performance, reduction in the number of errors, better visibility of data exchanges between the MDM system and the rest of the system. A static MDM system, not having at its disposal the management of the business states, is unable to benefit from such a rationalization of data synchronizations.

5.4. The MDM maturity model

Figure 5.1 represents the MDM maturity model, according to the virtual, static and semantic levels that have been described. The difference between a static MDM and a semantic MDM system is considerable. The strategic expectations are not the same; the effort required in data modeling and the acquisition of business knowledge are not comparable.

A virtual MDM system remains an IT solution. It rationalizes the development required to access data spread across several databases.

A static MDM system does not bring with it any real data governance as it is not based on validation rules expressed in a formal manner. This MDM is sufficient for IT as long as the data structures managed remain simple, as in codes and labels (reference data rather than master data), without any significant links to the business objects which form the heart of the Information System. This MDM system is dangerous because it necessitates bespoke software developments to implement data validation rules outside the data repository.

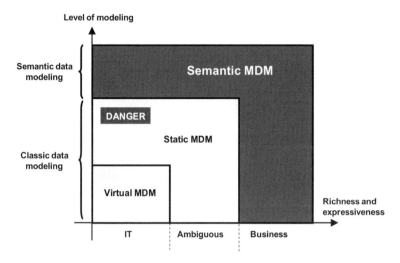

Figure 5.1. *The MDM maturity model*

A semantic MDM system offers the only level of maturity that interests business users. It goes together with the total re-appropriation of the knowledge of the data, using the formal expression of business states which govern the behavior of the business objects managed. The data model absorbs some of the data validation rules, which reduces the number of bespoke software developments needed. With a semantic MDM system, business users must be able to distinguish between business objects' states and states related to organizational processes or workflow. IT practitioners have little chance of correctly identifying these two levels of states. To achieve this, an understanding of the business beyond IT is required. Unfortunately, business users often express their knowledge via a computer system, already supposedly understood by IT specialists who in turn think, incorrectly, that they know the business better than their users! Unless the company finds an exit route from this way of working, an MDM system can only reproduce a part of the useless complexity coming from the existing functional and technical silos. This complexity is kept alive, not because of objective reasoning but out of habit, in the definition of business requirements and then implemented by IT specialists. These needs reproduce the weaknesses of the existing system without even realizing it because they seem unsolvable, as though genetically inherent to the company, which of course they are not.

What is at stake in a semantic MDM system is scope. As it purports to bring truth to the management of reference and master data, it cannot but help to also extract the weaknesses accumulated, sometimes over many decades in the development of functional and technical silos. It imposes a takeover of business knowledge, through the states of the business objects. Business users must describe the behavior of their IS Assets formed by their reference and master data, in a way that is not reliant on existing IT tools. IT experts, in the process of assisting in the statement of requirements, must supply the methodology and IT solutions to achieve this, i.e. guarantee a formal management of these business objects' states with the help of models.

In the end, the maturity of semantic MDM lies in a methodical approach rather than in the MDM software tool itself. Of course, if the tool assists in the definition and management of the business objects' states, then the method is better understood by those involved in the process. Nevertheless, if the tool contributes nothing at this level it has to be enhanced in order to manage the business objects' states as master data[3].

---

3. In practical terms, this means implementing a decision table per business object which states, according to the business states, the update permissions for each data element.

5.5. A *Model-driven* MDM system

In the first chapter of this book, we explained the difference between a "transactional data repository" and a "semantic data repository":

–   the first is based on a data model that does not accept validation rules. It corresponds to the classic relational database, similar to the maturity of a static MDM system;

–   the second is based on a rich data model which governs the behavior of the data repository thanks to the validation rules available in the model. This corresponds to a semantic MDM system, which can also be described, using its technical label, as a Model-driven MDM system.

Model-driven MDM completes the normal functionality of RDBMS (Relational Database Management System) with two notable additions that we will now describe: the management of data variants and a hiding mechanism for join tables. Even if this is somewhat technically advanced, it must be understood by business users as its implementation is key to the success of an MDM system process.

5.5.1. *Variants*

The same data model can contain different characteristics depending on variations linked to the context in which it is used. For example, a data element for a business object may be mandatory according to whether it is used by head office, a subsidary company, a partner, etc.

Rather than fix the information that specifies the mandatory parts of the data element, Model-driven MDM treats it as master data whose value (mandatory or optional) depends on the context in which the data model is being used[4].

This management of variants also applies to data cardinality which links the business objects to each other. For example, a Product is associated with zero to one Factory (0.1) in a first context of use (head office) and the same Product is associated with one to five (1.5) Factories when used in a different context (subsidiary).

Rather than using hard-coded programs to implement this integrity rule, an Model-driven MDM system manages these relational links as master data. So, the data model is configured from a series of meta-data which affects its behavior according to the context in which it is used.

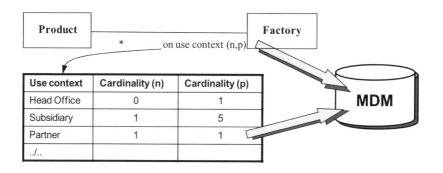

Figure 5.2. *Illustration of data cardinality variants*

5.5.2. *Hiding join tables*

Join tables are common in data models. They allow links between two or more business objects while avoiding duplication of information. For example, an employee is enrolled in several courses and the enrollment of several

---

4. This type of data can be described as "meta-data" because it impacts the behavior of the data model itself.

employees on the same course is possible. The join table is a technical object positioned between "employee" and "course". This object contains the list of employee identifiers and course identifier pairs showing the enrollments. This object, which only contains IDs, is not meaningful for the business by itself.

From a semantic point of view, it is preferable to say that employees are enrolled on courses and vice-versa. The technical object should not be visible to the business users and IT professionals are generally responsible for putting hard-coded software mechanisms in place to hide it from view. A Model-driven MDM system automatically hides the existence of this object, which eases the use of that data by business users while still avoiding bespoke developments led by IT professionals[5].

Figure 5.3 illustrates this principle, in the case of the relationship between authors and their books. The left-hand part illustrates the use of the join table; the right-hand part shows the use of the direct association between the book and author. The generation of the user interface is automatic because there is no join table to hide. Beyond this, the Model-driven MDM system ensures integrity controls and the non-duplication of information, despite the absence of a join table.

---

5. This technical mechanism is known as a Data Access Layer (DAL) or, more precisely, Object Relational Mapping (ORM) with specialized frameworks like Hibernate. A Model-driven MDM system reuses this mechanism and applies it to reference and master data in order to ease the business administration of the data, hiding join tables in the User Interface and software (application interface or services) as their presence is not relevant to business users.

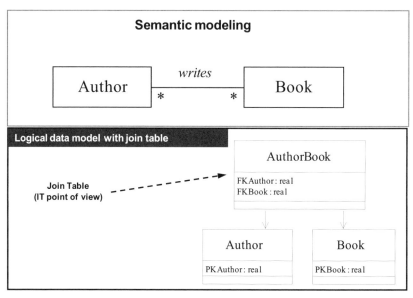

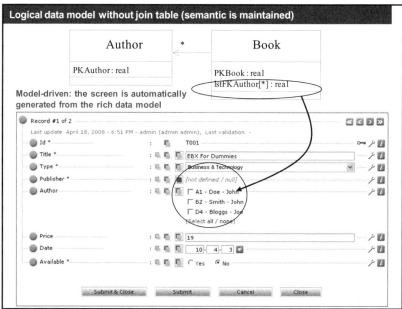

Figure 5.3. *Illustration of the hiding of join tables*

In this example, the association has been directed from the book to the author. It would also be possible to drive it from the other direction. There would thus be an additional user screen to manage this second path[6].

We have seen in this chapter that an MDM process must start at the highest level of maturity i.e. the semantic model, with its technical expression in the form of a Model-driven MDM system. Thanks to the semantic approach, the administration functions brought by MDM are delivered automatically to business users while limiting the hard-coding of software. We will now describe those functions in the following chapter.

---

6. The screen presented in this example is generated by a Model-driven MDM EBX platform from Orchestra Networks. The ergonomics retained is that of a list of check boxes; it is also possible to drive the generation of the screen in order to obtain other ergonomic representations, for example, as a list box.

Chapter 6

Data Governance Functions

The term "governance" is applied to several areas of management of organizations and IT systems. At its base, governance relates to the rules that describe the relationship between the stakeholders of a company, that is to say its employees, its managers, its third parties, its board of directors, its shareholders and public authorities.

In our context, governance applies to the management of an Information System in order to clarify the relationship between business users and their IT department, but also to support the IS and its underlying IT systems transformation.

We describe the "governance of reference and master data" firstly by its business functions, laid out in this chapter. The organizational aspects are dealt with in Chapter 7.

6.1. Brief overview

Before going into a complete description of each function of governance, we have summarized them with the help of

Table 6.1, in the order in which they are presented in the remainder of this chapter.

Function	Definition
Ergonomics (section 6.2)	Unified user interface for all data repositories.
Version management (section 6.3)	Creation of a version of the data, for example the description of a product. Automatic detection of the difference between versions and the possibility of merging the data from one version to another.
The initialization and update of data depending on use context (section 6.4)	Different enrichment of data depending on the context in which it is used as, for example, multi-language, multi-channel, geographical sectors, etc. The use contexts are created by the business users of the MDM system who have the appropriate rights, without modification of the data model.
Management of concepts related to time (section 6.5)	The management of data history, definition of period of validity applied to data, etc.
Validation rules (section 6.6)	Checking that any update on data is in line with validation rules. This function of governance is very important as it ensures the integrity and quality of the reference and master data.
Data approval process (section 6.7)	Co-ordination between MDM users involved in the update of data. This relates to a workflow with a task list by user.
Permission management (section 6.8)	Definitions of read only and update rights on data. These rights relate to subset of data, data elements and use cases, etc. A function allows the delegation of these rights to users in a collaborative way of working, for example between head office and subsidiaries.
Data hierarchy management (section 6.9)	Automatic examination of the data model to compute the links dependency between the business objects and data hierarchy management.

Table 6.1. *The list of governance functions applied to reference and master data*

The functions listed in Table 6.1 are made available by an MDM system through a user interface for business users, and by application program interfaces that ensure the integration of the data repository with the rest of the IT systems.

6.2. Ergonomics

The governance functions must be the same for all the users of an MDM system and all the data repositories. Whether it is for the administration of a product catalog, an organization or a chart of accounts, the MDM system user interface must be identical.

By contrast, if a company adopts different ergonomic approaches according to the data repository used there are several constraints that have to be dealt with which can compromise the MDM approach:

– additional costs for the design, implementation and maintenance of the different user interface for each data repository, although the governance functions are the same;

– a breakdown in the ergonomics as soon as one data repository, with one ergonomic structure, has to connect to another data repository which has a different ergonomic structure. For example, a product catalog states links between the data repository for the organization (the factories that make the products) and employees (the players in charge of the products). If these three data repositories are based on different ergonomic structures, the way of linking them is not natural, due to the diverging ergonomics.

The corollary of the previous point is the risk of the appearance of MDM silos; this means the temptation to duplicate a part of the data repository from factories and employees directly in the product catalog data repository.

This is one way of overcoming the ergonomics issues, but it leads to a risky and costly duplication of data.

It is better that a company uses the ergonomics provided by the MDM tool rather than embark on a specific project which would take time before the business agreed on a common ergonomic approach. Nevertheless, it should be possible to extend the ergonomics by default to better respond to certain needs. The capacity of an MDM tool to adapt its screens should be taken into account in any criteria for choosing a solution.

This approach takes advantage of the Model-driven MDM system, as the user interface is generated automatically by the tool, on the basis of a homogeneous ergonomic approach. As soon as the data model has been validated, the screens and the governance functions are also available without recourse to any specific software developments. In the remainder of this chapter, the governance functions retain the principle of a homogeneous ergonomic structure and conform to the approach of the Model-driven MDM.

6.3. Version management

Reference and master data is often enhanced over time, according to successive versions. For example, the description of a product can have a first version, enhanced over time according to the way the product evolves. A company keeps these versions for various reasons, such as for:

– regulatory reasons. At any time a company must be able to supply the values for certain data in a particular format. This need is common in the area of insurance products or the classification of financial assets;

– concurrent versions. This allows a business to work with different versions of the same data. For example, the same process of enrollment in a contract for medical assistance changes according to the legislation in force; several versions may co-exist for a certain time, according to the conditions laid down by business regulations;

– version control. The audit of data takes advantage of the difference in values according to the versions. For example, it is useful to examine the differences between the classification of two versions of financial operations. The audit of these differences allows the detection of unusual changes which can reveal irregularities;

– version merging. With two versions it is possible to copy some modifications on to the other. For example, a new version of a product description is built for the needs limited to a test environment. Once the tests have been completed, one part of the new values tested have to be merged with the current version used in production. By avoiding double entry of common data from one version to another, the risk of error is reduced, helping to give better data quality.

Version management is therefore an indispensable function to guarantee data quality. In its absence, it is necessary to physically duplicate the data repository in as many versions, with synchronization and merging issues to be resolved on a case by case basis using specific technical and programming procedures.

By contrast, an MDM system allows version management under the control of the business users of the data repository, on condition that they possess the appropriate access rights. This management is similar to that of more technical versioning of software. So, we find similar concepts of a reference branch and sub-branches. Each branch contains versions which are isolated in relation to the other branches.

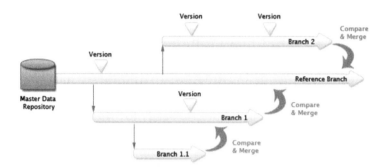

Figure 6.1. *Version management using the branches principle*
(copyright Orchestra Networks)

A user can create a "test" branch to configure a specific version of data without it modifying the current version for the same data, situated on the reference branch. Once the test has been completed, the user merges the test branch with the reference branch to retrieve all or part of the new data configuration, and then finally creates the new current version (see Figure 6.1).

6.4. The initialization and update of data by use context

Among the needs for data initialization and update by use context, the management of languages is the most classic. For example, the description of a product or error messages depend on the language in use. At the time of reference and master data entry, the user of the MDM system must know for which context, in this case language, the initialization or update is for.

Contexts diversify in order to take into account aspects such as subsidiaries, distribution channels, partners, etc. At the same time, data which is likely to be managed according to use context increases. This data not only concerns the tables of codes or labels but also complex data types like tariffs, regulations, organizations, etc. The effect of the globalization of the marketplace, of distributed working, and electronic communication explains the increasing importance of use context. They can appear at any time during the normal activity of a company. Equally, the data concerned by this type of management by use context are very volatile. To support this activity, it is important that the data repository is able to ensure the following functions:

– the users of the MDM system can, as long as they have the appropriate rights, create and delete use context as required, without it being necessary to change the data model or software. The use contexts are themselves master data administered by the MDM system;

– all data is susceptible to be managed through use context. Consequently, at the time of data modeling, it is not necessary to determine which are candidates for this type of management.

We will now describe how use contexts relate to each other, in the form of affiliation, and subsequently how to take advantage of this to automatically detect values common to several use contexts.

6.4.1. *The affiliation of contexts*

Contexts are not always independent in relation to each other. It is sometimes useful to manage them as hierarchies, according to an affiliation.

Here is a real example taken from a consumer credit card management company. The IT platform of this company is completely configurable with the help of a great deal of reference and master data which relates to the process of credit card enrollment. According to the partner that sells the cards, sometimes in a white label approach, the conditions of the discounts, the conditions of sale and the conditions of use of the card are customized.

In their MDM system, the company firstly manages a default value in the data repository. From this value, as many use contexts as partners are created. Each of these contexts inherits values by default and a customization is possible for each partner. For example, if data must respect a value range of between 1 and 100, each child context inherits this range and can change it, still respecting the minimum and maximum values without changing the values in the other contexts.

At any time, the business users have at their disposal a reporting tool which shows the differences between the default data repository and that updated by a partner. Also, some data are updated permanently, by the default data repository and are not able to be updated in the data repository by context.

At this stage, we have a default data repository, a first line of affiliation by context which represents the customization by the partners; and this affiliation continues. The business users give update rights on certain reference and master data to their partners' business teams. These teams access a part of the MDM system via an extranet, with access rights allowing them to create contexts in the affiliation of their own company, while this is invisible to other companies. A partner's business teams can also include their own distribution channels such as agency, internet and call center. According to these channels, certain reference and master data can be customized, on the condition that the organization owning the MDM system (parent company) delegates the necessary rights to the partner (see Figure 6.2). The parent company has at its disposal the knowledge of the contents of the all contexts and may impose on its partners a validation phase of the customizations, prior to use on the IT platform in a live environment.

The affiliation of contexts is an important concept. It avoids the unnecessary and dangerous physical duplication of the data repository. In our example, instead of a copy and paste of as many data repositories as partners, the MDM system administers a single repository with affiliations which contain the customizations.

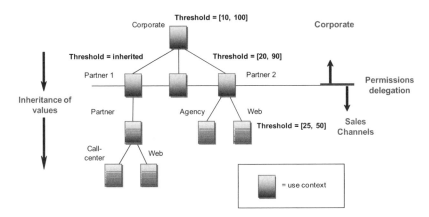

Figure 6.2. *Context management*

6.4.2. *The automatic detection of shared data*

The management of contexts also allows the analysis of existing data repositories so as to detect, automatically, the level of possible fatorization of data.

For example, we experienced the case of a regionalized bank whose current data repository, prior to the implementation of MDM, was duplicated by a simple copy and paste, as many times as there were regional offices. As the number of branches was high, around forty, these duplications presented serious issues of quality. An update of one data element, prior to being applied to all branches, was subject to a costly IT procedure updating forty databases. Over time, the bank found it difficult to keep track of the local branch updates; the comparison of the differences between each branch required computerized procedures which did not exist.

When this bank put in place MDM, the data repository of each branch was loaded in one MDM context, as previously described. The forty data repositories thus found themselves under the control of the MDM governance functions, with forty or so contexts. Thanks to the mechanism for comparing contexts, the MDM system automatically detected that only about 20% of the reference and master data was customized across all branches. The 80% remained common across all branches.

A context, by default, father of all the contexts of the branches, was put in place so as to group common data initializations and updates. Each branch context inherits default values and modifies certain data particular to its region, that is to say approximately 20% of the total of all reference and master data values. The regionalized bank now has, thanks to MDM, a better view on its regional updates and can feed, with greater quality, its sales and marketing strategy with the branches. When a data element which is common to all branches has to be updated, it is done directly at the highest level of the context and this value then applies itself automatically to all the data repositories of the branches via an automatic propagation mechanism.

6.5. Time management

Data can be updated differently in time. This is a requirement that must not be confused with version management; the differences are the following:

– a version affects the complete scope of the data repository, for example the data repository for "organization" or "products", etc. In the same version, clearly defined data elements must be updated differently according to time period. For example, a tariff discount has values which depend on the year quarter. The use of versions in the data repository for this requirement would not be appropriate as we are interested in one piece of data;

—   the creation of a version is not necessarily linked to the notion of time. For example, the creation of a working branch to test a new configuration of the data repository is not linked to the time management.

In the same way, the use of data updates by use context is not suitable because it is necessary to create as many contexts as time periods. This would make no sense and would bastardize the normal usage of context which is more oriented to taking into account geographical and organizational structures.

Neither must the management of time be confused with the audit trail function. This tracks, in a log, the different values which the data hold over time, associating with them information such as the user or the system from which the update originated. The audit trail records all updates and read accesses of all data in the order in which they take place in the database. There is no specific audit trail for each data element.

Having separated the ambiguities between versions, contexts and audit trails, we can now detail the principles of time management, firstly via the function of data history tracking and then the management of the business transactions, and finally the periods of validity.

6.5.1. *Data history tracking*

Data history tracking consists of saving, systematically, all the values assumed by a particular data over time. It is a kind of audit trail but applied to the scope of only one data element. For example, an insurance company must save all updates to contracts as legislation imposes this form of traceability.

In an MDM data repository, each object is described in the form of a header initialized at the time of creation, and a body of data that is subject to tracking. The data in the header which are frozen at the time of creation do not need to be tracked. This header contains in particular the business object's identifier and its creation date. Other information can be included, for example, the user's identifier or system from which the creation originated. Following this, each update of the business object occurs by an insertion of data in its body associated with the date of update. In this case, the MDM system does not allow the update of data and permits only creations and insertions.

This principle is applied systematically and prevents, for example, attempts to defraud which could happen with direct data updates. Data deletion follows the same principles and is enforced through a logical data deletion only, not though a physical deletion.

This data history tracking can prove more complex when associations between data have to be taken into account. Taking our previous example further, we can see that our business object "contract" is associated with a list of "guarantees". The behavior of the MDM system at the time of the update of a guarantee that is already attached to certain contracts has to be decided: should there be an automatic contracts history or not when modifying its guarantees? The reply to this question lies in the business requirements. Specification must be applied with care so as to adapt the behavior of the MDM system as required.

6.5.2. *Business transaction*

This function allows us to link all the updates resulting from a same user operation. For example, during the set up of a new contract, the MDM system user might first configure the new guarantees needed by this contract, before going on to configure it.

If only data tracking is used, it is not necessarily easy to know that the update of the guarantees was made in the context of the configuration of a contract. To overcome this issue, the MDM system must include the concept of "business transaction" which covers all updates that take place in a certain scope, more precisely the context in which it was used.

In our example, the MDM system should not see the update of the contract as separate from the update of the guarantees: the business transaction takes into account both the updates to the contract and the guarantees. To obtain this grouping, the MDM system passes the update date of the business transaction to all the updates of business objects involved at the heart of the transaction. In this way, the updates to the contract and guarantees are given the same time stamp. In this way, it is then easy to find all the linked updates.

6.5.3. *Validity period*

The validity period specifies at what moment the data is valid. For example, a discount rate is only available during a marketing campaign. The period can be limited to a start date. For example, an option for a product is described in the MDM system and becomes valid from a date fixed in advance.

The same data element can be associated with several periods of validity with different values according to different periods. For example, a discount rate can be different according to the year quarter and updated in advance at the beginning of each year. A tariff calculation queries the MDM system to retrieve the discount rate for a given date, in the future if it is for a price simulation or in the past if it relates to a historical price calculation.

It is at the time of data modeling that the decisions relating to the structure of the periods of validity must be made. They constitute, in themselves, master data that has to be administered by the MDM system. Consequently, if the discount rate is associated with four periods which relate to quarters of the year, the MDM system should automatically suggest a user interface that takes into account the four fields allowing the capture of the discount rate by quarter. As with each data element administered by the MDM system, this rate can be updated differently according to the versions of the data repository and the use contexts in each version. In this way it is possible, for example, to enter interest rates by quarter depending on the context of partner, subsidiary, geographical sectors, etc.

6.6. Data validation rules

At the time of data entry, the MDM system checks the validity of the updates. To do this, it executes data validation rules which were specified at the time of data modeling. These rules are independent of organizational issues, that is to say the permission management and data approval processes (for these functions, see later in this chapter).

It is necessary to distinguish three levels of data validation rules: facets, integrity constraints and business rules.

The more that these rules are specified in the data model the more a Model-driven MDM system is able to automatically take them into account which limits the bespoke developments outside the MDM system.

6.6.1. *Facets*

A facet expresses a constraint which relates to the format of a data element. If the format is not respected at the time of data entry, for example the omission of an email address domain, the MDM system refuses the update.

A facet can also express a constraint relative to a certain behavior of the data. In particular, while dealing with a list of data, it is often necessary to take into account a minimum and maximum number of occurrences. For example, an employee can have a minimum of two skills and a maximum of five. The MDM user can not go outside these limits: he must choose no less than 2 and no more than five skills for each employee. The MDM system manages the values in these limits as master data elements and automatically ensures compliance at the moment of data update.

In fact, these facets are described in the data model itself. An MDM system is able to execute them, automatically, without bespoke developments. The reliability of the data repository is thus strengthened because it is aligned with the data model which holds these facets.

Because these limit values are also master data, it is possible to update them differently according to the versions and the use contexts. In this way it is possible to configure the data in such a way that the minimum limit is equal to two skills for the subsidiaries and three for head office.

At the time of entering the skill, according to whether the data entry is in the context of a subsidiary or head office, the validation carried out by the facet is automatically adapted. The facet applies the minimum and maximum limits in relation to the context.

6.6.2. *Integrity constraints*

Integrity constraints are expressed in the data model. They are automatically taken into account by the MDM system at the time of data validation.

It is possible to distinguish three types of integrity constraint: enumerations, referential integrity constraints and business states.

6.6.2.1. *Enumeration*

An enumeration lays down that the value of a data element is retrieved from a list of pre-established values. For example, the color of a product is selected from a list (red, green, blue). This list is itself a master data element. Consequently it benefits from the same governance functions as versions or use contexts. In this way it is possible to define different lists of color by context. At the time of choosing a color for a product, the MDM system displays the list according to the management of use contexts. For example, if the context corresponds to geographical zones, updates can be language dependent: [*red, green, blue*], [*rot, grün, blau*], etc.

We have already seen that the contexts are not described in the data model. The governance functions of the MDM system allow us to configure more contexts dynamically, provided that we have the appropriate permissions.

6.6.2.2. *Referential integrity constraints*

Referential integrity constraints are expressed in the data model through associations between business objects. For example, if a Product is attached to at least one Factory, it appears in the data model as a "one to many" relationship (1.n) between product and factory. At the time of entry or update of a product, the MDM system forces the user to attach at least one factory code to it.

If necessary, the MDM system allows us to set up a specific governance function which is not available to all users, which nullifies all or part of the referential integrity constraints. This might prove necessary to facilitate the entry of certain data or the time of automatic data load. The MDM system has, in addition, a function through which a report detailing all the cases where the referential integrity constraints of the database have not been respected.

The data cardinality is also managed in the form of master data in the MDM system. This allows the referential integrity constraints to be customized with a simple parameterization, according to the use contexts, without modifying the data model.

6.6.2.3. *Business states*

In the previous chapter, dedicated to the maturity model of the MDM system, we have already mentioned the importance of the modeling of the lifecycle of the business objects and the use of the business states to enforce data validation rules. The objective is to prevent forbidden data updates due to the business objects' states' values. These states are also master data elements. A decision table is put in place, for each business object, which allows us to specify the constraints through the states which affect the data updates: this table details the data of the business object which can be modified for each state.

The entry of the decision tables happens in the same way as for other master data. Consequently, it is possible to allow several different updates for the same decision table, according to the versions and use contexts which have to be taken into account.

At the time of update of a business object, the MDM system automatically uses the decision table for this object in order to validate the update requested. This decision table is indispensable if the integrity of the MDM system is to be preserved. Even if, at first, a data analyst judges the decision table to be of no use, with little added-value, it is strongly recommended that it is kept. The interest is two-fold:

– first, it forces the implementation of an automatic procedure that uses the decision table. In this way its use is stabilized, verified and available for later use;

– secondly, it allows us to take a critical view at the basis of the modeling in which the business objects' states do not influence the update constraints of their reference and master data. This situation is not healthy when complex business data such as products, organizations, statements of accounts, real estate stocks, etc. are being managed.

6.6.3. *Business rules*

Business rules, the third level of data validation functions, after facets and integrity constraints, completes the group. These rules cannot always be expressed completely within the data model. Here are some examples of rules:

– when validating a product: "the product must contain one element whose weight exceeds half that of the total weight of the product";

– when validating a contract: "the contract must contain at least two guarantees from those available except in the case where an umbrella guarantee is selected and covers one of the two guarantees above";

– when entering a building (real estate stock): "in relation to the surface rented, the number of balconies and other master data, a calculation rule is used to suggest to the MDM user an automatic classification of the property from a dozen available. The user may modify the proposal given by the MDM system, on condition that he fills in a comment justifying his choice".

Two questions need to be covered. How do we determine the moment at which the rule is activated, and how is it executed? The place in which the activation of the rules is specified is determined by the Model-driven MDM system: it is naturally the data model which is in charge. To do this, the data analyst puts a condition on the data to which the rule applies. This condition specifies the exact moment at which the rule is enforced: before update, after update, after deletion, etc. In this way, the model contains the conditions to engage the correct rules according to the actions being carried out on the data. The rules are not necessarily placed in the model itself. More precisely, the use of a Service Oriented Architecture (SOA), allows the rules to be encapsulated as services launched through conditions declared within the data model. In this way the separation of the data in relation to the rules is ensured[1].

The way in which rules are executed is a more delicate question. If nothing has been planned, it is probable that the IT department will fill the gap with a classic software development which is not accessible to users. Such a software development prevents access to the rules by the users, which reduces the efficiency in management. Of course, if the number of data validation rules is limited, in particular during the first implementation of the data repository, it is possible to content oneself with this approach.

Nevertheless, to compensate for the hard-coded development of rules, the data repository must be associated with a sister solution which has the same governance objectives as the MDM system, but in the domain of business

---

1. In order to achieve this, a standard XML schema must be used and extended in order to take into account the declaration of associations between business objects and the launching of data validation rules. For an example, look at the Orchestra Networks' Model-driven MDM EBX software tool.

rules. This means a rule management system, in other words a BRMS. The rules, like those above, are expressed in a language which is almost natural, in terms understood by the business users. In the BRMS, the rules are subject to management principles similar to that of the MDM system, most notably in terms of version management, uses context management and traceability.

The coupling of the data repository and the rules management system allows the first (MDM) to query the second (BRMS) at the moment of validation or calculation of a data element. The technical infrastructure allowing this type of interaction is put in place through an IT platform the same size as the whole Information System. The business users control the data repository and the system managing the rules, allowing them to completely configure the management and validation of the reference and master data.

Over and above the management of the business rules, the MDM system must also deal with the rules linked to the organization, that is to say the approval process of the data and the management of access rights. We will now cover these two aspects.

6.7. The data approval process

The modification of a reference or master data element, apart from business validation, can also require the implementation of validation at an organizational level. This means a data approval process, that is to say a workflow which co-ordinates the actors involved in the validation of data.

For example, in a repository of financial structures, used for the consolidation of financial operations, a first actor creates a classification key which will enhance an existing structure. This master data element is, firstly, validated from a business point of view by a rule which specifies that the level of the classification does not exceed a certain depth. Once this validation has been checked, the new classification key is present in the data repository, but it finds itself under the control of a data approval process. As long as this process has not been completed, the data is not considered to be available to the users of the data repository. After the validation from the business point of view, this data approval process has automatically delivered a validation request to a manager of the organization. This validation is at an organizational level; it implies the intervention of a manager who gives or does not give approval. If the agreement is given, the master data element is validated. If not, according to the organizational requirements, either the update is canceled, and/or a request for modification is sent to the user responsible for data entry.

The MDM system allows the modeling of the data approval process and its automatic execution, without any IT software development. It relates to the usual workflow concept and tool already well known within companies.

6.8. Access rights management

As with all data management systems, an MDM system allows the management of access rights at all levels within the data repository, like, for example, access to a group of data, to a particular data element, or to all occurrences of the same data object corresponding to a certain selection criteria, etc. The configuration of access rights is dealt with by a data repository which re-uses the governance functions brought by the MDM system.

All the governance functions of the MDM system, like version control and management of use contexts, are subject to the management of access rights. For example, an MDM user is or is not authorized to create a new version, or to create new contexts etc.

One point not be overlooked concerns the function of the delegation of rights. We have already cited an example in this area. A credit card management company wants to delegate a part of the management of its data repository to the team responsible at one of its partners who sometimes distribute cards using a white label approach. Thanks to this delegation of rights, a user account is made available to the manager at the partner which allows access to the MDM system, with access limited to his data and limited governance functions; for example, version control and access to audit trails are not available.

This delegation of rights can also be used between business users and IT department so as to distribute responsibilities according to the type of data and the choice of organization. In particular, a business unit may want to delegate the management of certain reference and master data to its IT department. In the same way, within the IT department, project teams might delegate the administration of certain technical reference and master data, such as the configuration of the technical infrastructure (firewall, system parameters, etc.), to the team specialized in IT production.

6.9. Data hierarchy management

Semantic modeling allows us to obtain a rich data model providing much information on the relationships between business objects. These relationships are important in order to use the reference and master data in a reliable and efficient way. For example, it is of strategic importance to find out if the same person is applying for several credit cards under different names, as a private individual, on behalf of his company, through a parent, etc.

In order to make the most of these relationships, already contained in the data model, the calculation of data dependencies is a governance function which allows them to be scanned automatically in order to carry out an impact analysis and to put forward ways of querying the data. For example, in a data model, an Article is linked to a Product which is in turn linked to a Catalog, a Region, and a Factory. It is possible to query the articles by product and catalog, or by region and even by factory.

It is also possible to combine several of these dependencies (or axes of dependencies).

Rather than build data dependencies from scratch, a Model-driven MDM system has at its disposal a rich data model which allows it to automatically take advantage of the relationships between business objects. From the moment that the model is available, the data dependencies are automatically calculated and querying the data according to different hierarchies of values is possible. More than this, the user, if they have the rights, can extend the calculated data dependencies by adding other attributes present in the business objects concerned, as, for example, the date of the article; a query of articles by product, catalog, month, quarter and year is thus obtained. It is also possible to add sort criteria, or filters on the attributes of the data objects queried, etc. In the end, the calculation of the data dependencies and the consultation of the hierarchies allow a complete and powerful querying of the reference and master data.

6.10. Conclusion

Arriving at the end of this chapter, we can understand that an MDM system offers governance functions that are both rich and complete. Others exist and have not been described here through lack of space: access to the audit trail, data modeling tools, parameterization of the data exports, etc.

Now we must follow up the subject of the governance and concern ourselves with the organization surrounding an MDM system. In particlular, it is necessary to specify the roles of the actors who control the governance functions. The following chapter is entirely dedicated to this aspect.

Chapter 7

Organizational Aspects

In the previous chapter, we dealt with governance functions brought by the MDM solution. We will now follow up this study from an organizational point of view, concentrating on the relationship between business users and their IT department.

Without a strategy with sponsorship from the highest level, the organization which we describe here has little chance of seeing the light of day. It requires a high level of business commitment which can only be justified by a company-wide objective; it concerns the valuation of intangible IS Assets embodied through business repositories. Two organizational aspects have to be taken into account: that which is necessary to encourage and support the reference and master data modeling and the definition of the roles surrounding the management of data.

7.1. Organization for semantic modeling

All too often, the approach adopted by business users during the specification of requirements is informal. When models are used, it is with a conceptual analysis approach, far removed from the precise description of data and associated validation rules that are, in fact, required. At best they express generalities which establish the high level aims of what the future system might look like, with sometimes detailed rules, but which cover only part of the requirements. In most companies, these models contain data duplication, are ambiguous and incomplete. IT specialists cannot use them exactly as they are to design programs. Instead, they have to complete them and distort them, which lead IT practitioners to detail what should have been done at the business level. Thus, IT teams try to replace their business users without having either the vocation or the skills.

The MDM approach cannot allow such a breakdown between the requirements and the build of the software. The alignment of the governance functions with the business requirements will not happen if this breakdown is not removed.

It is necessary to increase the modeling effort conducted by the business to support a repository driven by models, i.e. a Model-Driven MDM. Commitment to this model must be enshrined in the highest levels of the business management and, since MDM acts on data shared between different business units, it is necessary that the organization promotes the sharing of models.

But business users alone are not able to supply sufficient effort to achieve such an ambition in relation to modeling. If each business unit within a company designed its own data model, then the company would be faced with as many data models. Only executive management can supply sufficient impetus to demand the co-ordination required for the work involved in data modeling at the Information System level.

7.1.1. *The foundations of the organization*

From the outset, the objective of co-ordination of effort between business units presents a problem. The difficulties that the actors in the Information System must face are embedded in the company's organizational layout. The business units work with their own processes in a way that is isolated from the others, with their own Profit and Loss account. The taste for silos, unfortunate for IT systems, is already present in the genes of business management: marketing, sales, production, after sales, accounts, HR, etc.

Each business unit sees customers, products, financial structure and other information from its own point of view. These multiple points of view generate wide discrepancies in modeling. They are so embedded in the management culture of each business unit that it is difficult to find the commonality that is sought out in an MDM system. This effort should be nonetheless maintained and managers should not be discouraged. It is made even more difficult because IT itself maintains these unhelpful differences in the form of functional and technical silos trapping the same data in different technical structures. However, one must not believe that all reference and master data can be shared. Some of them are, quite legitimately, modeled specifically for the needs of one business unit. Intelligent modeling makes a distinction between what should be shared and that which remains specific to a particular business unit.

In this context, how must one proceed so as to agree with the different business units on a shared vision of common data? First, one must identify the data owners. For example, who is the owner of customer description: is it sales management or financial management? Next, it is necessary to put in place a transversal task force whose job is the co-ordination of the data modeling work itself. We will now detail these two aspects.

7.1.2. *Data owners*

Each reference and master data element is placed under the responsibility of a business unit or department (financial, customer care, HR, manufacturing, etc.). For example, in a company in the manufacturing sector, the business object "Contract" is under the responsibility of the manufacturing department, even though this data object is used and extended by other parts of the business, such as by Finance and Customer Services. The owner of the business object "Contract" is responsible for its data modeling. The other management teams must be involved, to take into account their needs and if necessary manage variants of this data modeling according to their requirements. The shared version for the data model "Contract" is thus situated in one place: the manufacturing department.

To be able to name data owners, one must have an enterprise architecture of reference and master data even before starting the modeling[1]. This data map defines the boundaries between the data that allows the distinction between the domains of the business objects and the business objects themselves. It is from these boundaries that "property titles" are established.

Two forms of organization are possible:

– multi-ownership is forbidden. In this case, each business object is the property of one business unit including that data which corresponds to the extensions specific to other units. The property title covers both common data and that which is specific to other business units;

– multi-ownership is allowed. In this case, the shared part of the business object is always under the responsibility

---

1. We will come back to the process of testing this landscape in Chapter 8.

of one business unit, but each extension is placed under the responsibility of the business unit which is its owner.

The two approaches must be evaluated carefully. The first is radical. The second is open and flexible. However, experience shows that it is preferable to adopt the first. In fact, the risk of trouble with the data modeling is higher with multi-ownership. This approach implies a monitoring to prevent the duplication of data elements between those which are common and those which are specific to one business unit. The temptation is very high for a business unit which is not owner of the common part to create its own data modeling field, even if the data should be common. Whatever the case, the map of the data and the property titles are under the responsibility of a transversal organization across the whole of the company: the Enterprise Data Office.

7.1.3. *The Enterprise Data Office*

The Enterprise Data Office department is attached to the executive management and does not report to the IT department. It fulfills the following functions:

– support and quality during the data modeling;

– guardian of the data map across the whole of the Information System;

– planning and budgetary control.

7.1.3.1. *Support and quality during the modeling*

The Enterprise Data Office oversees the modeling in order to head off problems that may arise in the data model. For example, modeling of the business object "Contract" can cater to the needs of those involved in the first round of negotiations but prove to be inadequate when used by a particular business unit.

If this type of problem is not anticipated, the data model is not sufficiently stable and frequent and incompatible versions will hamper the MDM approach.

The Enterprise Data Office also oversees the data dictionary, common across the company which defines business terms: customer, prospect, partner, turnover, place, etc. The Enterprise Data Office also intervenes when the business units are unable to reach an agreement about common data. It can then act in the role of assisting the negotiation and act as an arbitrator.

The Enterprise Data Office is the single point of contact for the reference and master data models and the data dictionary across the whole of the company. It can even, depending on the organization, be responsible for operational tasks during modeling and the initialization and maintenance of the data dictionary.

7.1.3.2. *Guarantor of the enterprise data map*

The Enterprise Data Office is responsible for the design of the enterprise data architecture (data map), common to the company, which delineates the scope in which the business objects are distributed by business units within the organization.

This enterprise data map is used to nominate the data owners. Important interdependencies between business objects are formalized early in the process, in order to identify the data which has the highest level of sharing between business units so that it can be modeled first. A roadmap, taking into account the modeling procedures and the priorities for the release of the data repositories, is written and maintained. This roadmap is under the responsibility of the Enterprise Data Office which updates it, during the progress of the MDM process.

7.1.3.3. *Planning and budgetary control*

The Enterprise Data Office is the point of contact for executive management to determine the investment plan for the data modeling and its follow up. Each business unit must establish its annual budget for data modeling by domains of reference and master data. This budget must highlight concrete and regular outcomes. One part of the investment is dedicated to the internal needs of the business unit, another to the shared effort with the other business units to encourage and support a common data modeling across the whole of the company.

The follow up of the plan is done by separating these two analytical keys in order to ensure that the business units follow the effort of the shared data modeling. Consequently the Enterprise Data Office assumes budgetary control of the dedicated funds, by business unit and for its own transversal activity.

7.1.4. *Does this organization involve risks?*

The organization that has just been described could be a worry to management in more ways than one. The subject of return on investment will be left to one side as it has already been covered (see Chapter 4). The other concerns relate to the four themes that will now be followed up:

– Is the mutualization of data modeling work dangerous?

– Do the business users have the correct skills to model?

– How are data models validated?

– What are the connections between this organization and the IT department?

7.1.4.1. *Is the mutualization of data modeling dangerous?*

Let us try to understand the risks surrounding the mutualization of the model using an example, that of the "Product" data repository. When a product is configured it must be attached to the factories which fulfill the criteria that fit its configuration.

In order to decide which factories to attach, the MDM system presents the user with a set of data concerning its workshops, its production capacity and other means of supply. The data model for the configuration of products is thus linked to another data model, that of the description of the factories.

The business object "Product" is under the responsibility of the "Product management" department and the business object "Factory" is under the responsibility of another business unit, that of the "Manufacturing department". The consequences of the lack of reuse of the "Factory" data model between these two business units will now be described, as will the consequences of its mutualization.

The Factory data model without mutualization

Without mutualization, the product data repository includes its own modeling for factories. This modeling is rich because it contains all the characteristics necessary for the selection of factories according to the configuration of the products. Data values for this model must be loaded by the factory data repository which is under the responsibility of the manufacturing department. This second data repository, due to the absence of mutualization in modeling, has its own data model. The IT function has then to put in place a data synchronization mechanism between the two models describing factories, the one included in the MDM "product" and that of the MDM "factory". IT has to synchronize the two separate databases even though the description of the factories could be common to both. The technical workload is evident to the business users, when managing the repositories, because the differences in the data models leads to information on the factories becoming de-synchronized: how can it be guaranteed that the MDM "product" has the latest description of the factories?

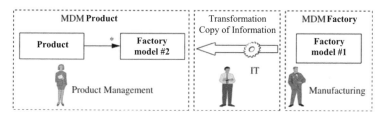

Figure 7.1. *Absence of mutualization in the factory data model*

The Factory data model with mutualization

At the opposite end of the scale, let us take a look at the situation where the actions of the Enterprise Data Office has lead to a mutualization of the Factory data model, valid for both the business unit "Product management" and "Manufacturing". In this case, the data repository "Product" presents to the user the information on the factories but in terms of "manufacturing" reference and master data. There is no longer a silo effect between the product description and the description of the factories. One unified data model is imposed on all the business units.

At the time of configuring a product, all the characteristics of the factories are not accessible. Read-only rights are managed by the MDM system which consequently filters the presentation of the factory data.

Over time, the shared Factory data model can become incompatible owing to evolving requirements. For example, let us imagine that a business regulation imposes a difference in the management of its offshore factories as opposed to those on national soil. In the offshore factories a group of additional data appears, such as specific criteria linked to the environment and working conditions. In this situation the mutualization of the factory model is either:

– a positive factor, as all the existing data repositories must conform with this new business regulation; or

– a problem, because it is preferable that the existing data repositories are not all aligned with this business regulation. For the MDM system in this case, it is necessary to ensure the co-existence of two different versions of the Factory data model and opt for the use of one or the other according to the data repository. Over time, the alignment of all data repositories to the same Factory data model is undoubtedly preferable so as to rationalize costs and increase data quality.

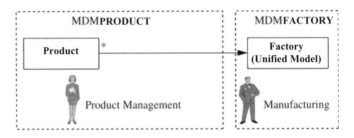

Figure 7.2. *Mutualization of the factory model*

In the end, it is generally less dangerous to mutualize the data modeling rather than to allow the differences in the shared reference and master data to increase. The level of useless complexity in the IT systems surrounding the silo effect shows this.

The lack of data traceability, auditability and flexibility are more damaging than the effort required to reach an agreement on the mutualization of common data.

7.1.4.2. Do the business users have the correct skills to model?

Business users need to have two types of skills at their disposal. The first should be a given. It relates to information knowledge management. All data used must have a precise meaning, the business objects' states must be well-described, the data validation rules specified. If this knowledge is not well grounded one should move quickly to the second skill, that of data modeling. In fact, it is only by modeling that business knowledge can be taken in hand.

Unfortunately, modeling skills are not recognized by business users and are not common in companies. It can be evaluated by the mastery of the knowledge modeling procedures, in particular when it applies to the core business itself, leaving to one side the organizational aspects such as workflows (business process) and permission management. It relates to semantic modeling, which will be covered in the last part of this book. Although this modeling calls for specific Information System skills it is important that the business users understand its use, as they must either carry it out by themselves or request experts in the IT department to collaborate with them in carrying it out.

The objective of semantic modeling is to represent in a formal manner, in the form of knowledge modeling, the business objects, their full descriptions and their inter-relations. The use of a standard language is a defining aspect. It has to be understood by all the players in charge of the Information System and its underlying IT systems, both business teams and IT experts. Rather than re-invent a proprietary language, the industry standard should be used, that is to say UML[2] or other DSL (Domain Specific Language).

---

2. Unified Modeling Language (UML) as standardized by the Object Management Group (OMG).

IT practitioners should accompany their business users in modeling. Often they act on behalf of the business users when the business does not have the scope to fully cover the task.

At the same time, the Enterprise Data Office also acts in the role of support and quality control.

During modeling, an opportunity arises to encourage knowledge sharing between participants. In particular, members of staff who have long and solid experience in the business, maybe who have previous experience in large IT projects relying on data modeling, should be appointed. Younger employees who are in the process of discovering the company should also be involved, so as to favor knowledge transfer. Finally, over and above the understanding of the modeling, a fundamental question is raised, that of the process of data models validation.

7.1.4.3. *How are data models validated?*

Validation of data models should be accessible to business users without much support from IT experts. Even if the data modeling can be outsourced to the IT Department, this is not true of data validation.

As owners of the data repositories, the business users must validate the data models otherwise the MDM system belongs only to the IT department. To get to this validation point using only data models is insufficient for two reasons:

– these models are difficult to understand by those who are not specialists in modeling and UML or other DSL;

– the actors responsible for the validation of the models are not only the ones who modeled them. This second group will almost certainly not have the necessary modeling skills to understand the models.

Consequently, it is necessary to find an indirect way to validate the data models, using prototyping in the form of a user interface to which business users can relate. To get to this point, a Model-driven MDM tool is unavoidable. All the data management screens are automatically generated from the data model. There should not be any heavy software development needed between the moment that the data model is available and the time that the screens (which can be understood by business users) are available. So one could say that the approach at our disposal is one of *"What you model is what you get"*. By handling data using the data governance functions brought by the MDM system, the underlying data model can be more easily validated by the business users. This model-driven approach is mandatory to involve business users in the validation of data models. Without this tool-based strategy for validation, business users cannot be owners of the data models or the data repositories on which they are based.

7.1.4.4. What are the connections between this organization and the IT department?

In order to succeed in data modeling with a real participation of business users, the IT department needs to be involved at several different levels. First, IT must put forward the semantic data modeling procedures as well as the tools to support the process (data modeling workshops, backup and security of the data models). Following on from this, IT must accompany business users and the Enterprise Data Office so that they can adopt the data modeling procedures and also so that they can use the MDM system as a tool for prototyping at the time of the data models validation.

In their own department, IT experts must translate the data models into the technical terms expected by the MDM software. IT architects have to handle the integration of the

MDM system with the rest of the Information System. This aspect will be covered in Part Three of this book.

7.2. The definition of roles

Several roles are required to be able to model the data and then govern it. Among these roles, that of data owner has already been identified. The others are new: data analyst, data architect, data cost accountant, and data steward.

7.2.1. *Data owner*

The data owner is responsible for the data's meaning, its validation rules, and its values. S/he represents the project supervisor for the data. Groups of data are assigned to the same owner, for example for the whole of a business object or even aggregations of several business objects. The owner is responsible for the validation of the data models which are assigned to them. These models are supplied by the actors in charge of the modeling (see the data analyst role). This validation takes place, thanks to a Model-driven MDM system, following a process of prototyping of screens.

The skills required by a data owner are those of the business field. S/he is not a data modeler. The data owner is also in charge of the financial evaluation of their master data. S/he must follow their stock of reference and master data and, in collaboration with the Enterprise Data Office, put in place tools to allow the data to be financially evaluated.

7.2.2. *Data analyst*

The data analyst is the actor who models the data. This entails project supervision on behalf of the data owner. The data analyst puts into practice the semantic data modeling procedures. Each business unit contains this role.

The IT department also has data analysts of a more technical kind. They have the role of accompanying the business analysts and of translating the semantic data models into a logical form and then into the technical terms necessary for the MDM software (see Chapter 10).

In practice, the data analyst role is often delegated to the IT department because the skills and means for modeling are rarely available within business units.

7.2.3. *Data architect*

The data architect is a pivotal role in the Enterprise Data Office, with a transversal function in relation to business units in order to ensure support and quality control. S/he oversees the evolution of the data models in order to anticipate any problems that might arise, intervening, as a last resort, to conduct arbitration on the modeling. The data architect's skill set is very wide. S/he must have a perfect understanding of the modeling procedures and have a good understanding of the different business functions in the company so as to able to become the key point of reference.

By establishing the data map (enterprise data architecture), the data architect allows the responsibilities of the data owners to be assigned. This role cannot be easily delegated to the IT department because the business units will then be unable to control, autonomously, the quality of the modeling operations across the whole of the Information System.

The data architect has an opposite number in the IT department; that person assists him in the execution of the data modeling procedures.

7.2.4. *Data cost accountant*

Under the control of executive management, the data cost accountant watches over the investment budget for the data modeling and, by business unit, follows its progression. S/he is also in charge of establishing the accounting principles for the financial asset evaluation of the reference and master data. S/he is either in the Enterprise Data Office or in that part of the organization already in charge of cost accounting.

7.2.5. *Data steward*

The data steward is the player who, in their daily activities, uses the governance functions brought by the MDM system. They report to the data owner. During the data approval processes, it is not unusual that the intervention of a data owner or one of his representatives be requested to validate updates carried out by the data steward.

In many companies, there are already teams specialized in the management of reference data and parameters, such as managing tariff tables, organizational structures, regulatory codes, etc. These teams fill a role which is similar to the role of data steward.

7.3. Synthesis of the organization required to support the MDM

Figure 7.3 summarizes the choice of organization for the modeling and management of reference and master data.

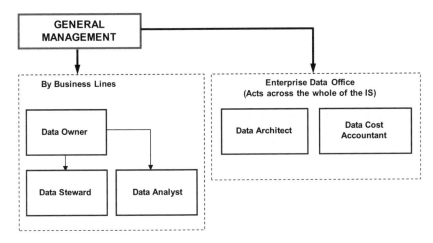

Figure 7.3. *The organization for the MDM process*

The conditions for success for an IT department are laid out in the remainder of the book, particularly in Chapter 12 which deals with the integration of the MDM system with other IT systems.

PART THREE

MDM from the
IT Department Perspective

Chapter 8

The Semantic Modeling Framework

This chapter outlines the framework of semantic modeling[1]. We will not return to the justification for the MDM approach, nor to its return on investment. We have already detailed these aspects in the previous parts of this book. Semantic modeling is based on UML which offers a standard and universal language to represent knowledge in information systems, and is consequently neutral vis-à-vis MDM tools.

8.1. Establishing the framework of the method

Semantic modeling is a separate discipline. Its object is to construct and maintain a knowledge base of a company's business, understandable by all actors involved in the Information System and its underlying IT systems. This type of modeling is positioned in a methodological framework which encompasses other disciplines, notably the analysis and design of organizations, logical modeling and technical architecture.

---

1. The detailed processes are described in the following chapter.

We will define the objectives of semantic modeling and then its application lifecycle. This will lead us to outline the method necessary to succeed with this modeling, which is indispensable in the MDM approach.

8.1.1. *The objectives of semantic modeling*

Semantic modeling allows us to represent knowledge independently from organizational concerns and IT solutions. To get to this point, the following principles are applied:

– separate the business lifecycle of the data from that of organizational processes;

– manage data integrity formally and completely;

– model in a way which is comprehensible to the business, with results that are stable and sustainable;

– model by separating technical constraints.

We will now detail each of these principles.

8.1.1.1. *Separate the business lifecycle of the data from that of the organizational processes*

The business lifecycle of data should not be confused with that which exists at the organizational level, often seen via a data updates approval process.

The expression "data governance" almost always makes reference only to the data approval processes. It hides the underlying business dynamic which regulates the behavior of the data at a business level, purged of all organizational situations. For the same business lifecycle for a data element it is possible to have several versions of approval according to the organizational variations.

The business integrity of the data is guaranteed thanks to the control of lifecycles at a business level. Even if the data update approval process malfunctions, the data in the system retains its integrity as long as the business lifecycles are respected.

If the concerns of the business and the organization are not separated, we run the risk of creating an MDM system with limited flexibility, even harmful in regards to the integrity of the data. In that case, an evolution in the organization would require an update which would have an impact on the MDM system at a business level even though it evolves following a different lifecycle.

8.1.1.2. *Managing data integrity*

To separate the business from the organization, it is necessary to identify the business state of each data element used over the course of time. In practice, this state is attributed to an aggregation of data grouped under a business object. In this way, according to the various states of the business object, updating is or is not possible. Certain updates will always be authorized, irrespective of the business object's states. By distinguishing the operations which are dependent on the business objects' states from those which are not dependent, the modeling is more rigorous, clear and protective of the data integrity.

If this distinction is not taken into account in the modeling, then we run the risk of authorizing data modifications without even realizing, early enough, the damage they cause to the integrity of the information. A static modeling of data, not taking into account the lifecycles of business objects, can lead to data modifications even though the business context does not enable it. It is therefore necessary to take a step back from the study of the data in order to find and counter the risks of the deterioration of integrity in the MDM system itself. Static modeling of the

MDM system can be insufficient to fix data integrity problems. Such an MDM system would therefore be completed by "hard coded" software developments, freezing the data validation rules that depend on the states.

8.1.1.3. *Modeling in a comprehensible, stable and sustainable manner*

The data models are structured progressively during the production of the MDM system. We will see that this approach, in stages, is based on a structure around three architecture levels that we call "business object domains", "data categories" and "business objects". In the absence of this distinction in the architecture, the sharing of data between actors and systems in the company becomes harder. Equally, the ability of the models to be extended or maintained is then harder to guarantee.

This structure is robust, negotiated and shared across the whole Information System, and even beyond if the data is being exchanged with other organizations. The detail of the data, inside each business object, can evolve depending on what is needed, but the structure forms a stable and sustainable asset. This architectural building gathers together disciplines varied in the methods, organization and knowledge of business. It is a multi-disciplinary task, unavoidable as soon as the aim is an implementation of an MDM system across the whole of the information system. We must ensure that its construction is achieved by best practices and that putting it in place occurs in a progressive manner.

8.1.1.4. *Modeling setting aside the technical constraints*

The MDM system provides the other systems with the reference and master data, either by replication of the data, or by a service mode access (see Chapter 12). Some data is updated by systems other than the MDM system. It is then necessary to envisage a synchronization process between the

MDM system and these systems, in a bi-directional way. In any case, the objective is to cut, as rapidly as possible, the updates of data in a "point to point" mode between systems, benefiting from an integration by the MDM system. In order to achieve this, the data integration layer (EAI, ESB, ETL) must be mastered by the company.

This technical integration is a project in its own right that IT must handle with care. Often, there is a strong temptation to take into account, in the data model, certain technical constraints justified by the connection mechanisms of the MDM system. For instance, if the best practices of the EAI limit the depth of the data types or forbid inheritance, this must not be taken into account during semantic modeling. The semantic model is a business model; it is a model of knowledge that is not constrained by the preoccupations of performance or implementation in the software. The technical constraints are regulated later on, in the translation of the semantic model to a logical data model, and at the time of the integration of the MDM system with the rest of the Information System. We will return to this in the following chapters.

8.1.2. *The lifecycle of semantic modeling*

The semantic modeling lifecycle can follow two paths, already known to companies, under the names of bottom-up and top-down. The first, interactive in nature, aims to build the data model by progressively revealing its foundations. The second, on the other hand, means that preparation work must first be carried out, in order to build the structure of the model before starting the detailed modeling of it. By making clear the benefits and constraints of these two approaches, we will show that they must be combined in order to successfully achieve semantic modeling.

8.1.2.1. *Bottom-up*

The use of a bottom-up approach is interesting in order to progressively validate the different model versions, built in stages. Due to the multiple and often short iterations brought by this lifecycle, the MDM system must be capable of rapidly exploiting the data models in order to automatically generate the necessary user interface for data governance. This MDM, based on models, corresponds to the Model-driven MDM (see Chapter 5).

The iterative approach means managing repeating cycles of data migration, from one data model version to another. The successive versions can impact the integration layer that synchronizes the MDM system with the rest of the IT system.

The lack of a global approach makes stable modeling (which sufficiently integrates a sustainable architecture frame early enough) more difficult. Consequently, the recommended use of the *bottom-up* approach is as follows:

– the iterative cycle is used with a view to prototyping the model, without a final loading of data. As soon as the iterations provide a stable version of the model, the data loading is carried out definitively. From then on, data model version management is compulsory and is accompanied by data migration procedures between versions;

– from the first iterations, the data model takes into account best practices that facilitate modifications in upward compatibility, which limit the burden of data migration from one model version to another, e.g. the use of complex types rather than simple ones, transversal domain-gathering reusable data types, dynamic attributes, etc.

The use of a single iterative approach is not recommended. It is necessary to benefit from the capacity to demonstrate and validate data models but it must be completed by a more global architecture, i.e. top-down, to reinforce the sustainability of data models.

Model-driven MDM and model validation

With Model-driven MDM, business users validate the data models under the form of a friendly user interface automatically generated by an MDM tool. The business users interact, at the time of each new data modeling iteration, with screens aligned with the latest data models. The validation of these screens does not affect the ergonomics generated, by default, by the MDM tool, but affects the data model itself. A Model-driven MDM system enables an agile design, implementation and validation process of the semantic model. Once the data model is validated, then the ergonomics generated by default can be adjusted depending on the requirements of the users.

This use of the MDM system can also be envisaged beyond the scope of reference and master data. It is often delicate, for the business teams and IT experts, to validate the UML data models with precision. This is why it is useful to have a tool capable of importing these models, in order to automatically generate screens enabling navigation throughout the entirety of the data, with the help of an ergonomy which is business friendly. A Model-driven MDM system supplies this facility.

8.1.2.2. *Top-down: Enterprise Data Architecture*

Making the effort to achieve global modeling ensures greater data model stability and a better upward compatibility of successive versions. Nonetheless, this "top down" approach requires a good knowledge of the business, and mastery of the modeling procedures. The objective is to establish a data architecture landscape map across the whole of the Information System, before detailed data modeling. This is an Enterprise Architecure approach applied to data.

The choice between the iterative lifecycle (bottom-up) and the Enterprise Architectural (top-down) approach is not specific to an MDM project. It is present in all modeling domains: reference and master data, transactional data, processes, etc. In most cases, to support a sustainable approach, the design of the rough components of the data architecture, across the whole Information System, must be agreed upon. These components organize the foundation of the data models. Then, in agreement with this foundation, the detailed modeling of data is done thanks to an iterative approach. In the end, this reconciliation of bottom-up and top-down approaches results in the following recommendations:

– proceed, as soon as the MDM project is launched, towards a modeling of the highest level architectural components, i.e. the business object domains and the identification of business objects within these domains. At this stage, you are not yet looking to model information that describes the content of business objects;

– this level of modeling is sustainable. If the semantic modeling procedures are mastered, there is no reason to modify the resulting architecture in depth; it is a solid and sustainable data foundation. Nonetheless, evolutions remain possible and follow a maintenance cycle involving a Enterprise Architecture responsibility across the whole

Information System (see Chapter 7). Decisions taken locally, within a project, must be forbidden, as soon as they modify the data foundation shared by the company;

– thanks to this Enterprise Architecture, applied to data, it is then easier to engage an iterative modeling of business objects, since the foundation is stabilized.

8.2. Choosing the method

With respect to the objectives that we have just set, it is now important to acquire a method that supplies the modeling procedures. Rather than re-invent an approach dedicated to the MDM system, we prefer to retain the Praxeme "open source" method. This method will provide us with a good overview of some required modeling procedures, even though others methods can fit with our approach.

8.2.1. *The Praxeme method*

The objectives and the modeling lifecycle that we have just described require the use of a method that leaves room, in its own right, for semantic modeling and for the Model-driven approach.

It is difficult and costly to perfect such a method: this is an objective that is out of the company's reach. Only the grouping of investments can guarantee a solid elaboration of the methodological procedures, their diffusion on a large scale and their maintenance. The Praxeme open source method responds to these demands. Its "Enterprise System Topology" (EST), in other words, its framework of description of the Information System, takes into consideration semantic modeling and standard Model-driven Architecture (MDA)[2]. Praxeme is the result of the joint investment of institutional

---

2. Standard of the OMG (Object Management Group).

contributors and individuals who act within the Praxeme Institute, a non-profit making institution, in the spirit of an open source community.[3]

The Praxeme method covers a large spectrum of modeling procedures for the expression of requirements and the design of Information Systems and IT systems. With regard to an MDM system, we use a subset of these procedures, completing and making clear their specific benefits for the management of reference and master data.

Our last book, *Sustainable IT Architecture: the progressive way of overhauling Information Systems with SOA* [BON 07], describes how the method is employed in a complete manner, beyond the reference and master data, and in particular for the progressive overhaul of IT systems based on Service Oriented Architecture (SOA).

Figure 8.1 presents a model of the "Enterprise System Topology"[4] which is formulated in UML language. The dotted arrows express the dependency links between "packages". Each package corresponds to an "aspect" of the IS topology, that is to say a point of view of the Information System.

The sections below present the modeling procedures applied to the MDM system, expressed in terms of the Praxeme method. In the MDA standard of the OMG, the upstream models (semantic, pragmatic and geographical) as well as the logical model are in the Platform Independent Model (PIM), i.e. independent of IT tools and infrastructure. The software model corresponds to the Platform Specific Model (PSM); it is dependent on the technical solution.

---

3. The complete documentation of the Praxeme method is available free at: http://www.praxeme.org.
4. Dominique Vauquier, author of the Praxeme method, is at the origin of this topology.

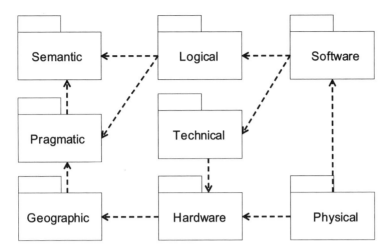

Figure 8.1. *Enterprise System Topology (EST) of Praxeme*
(creative commons)

8.2.1.1. *Semantic aspect*

Definition: semantic aspect

The semantic aspect is focused on the modeling of information that describes the core of the company business; i.e. in a manner which is independent of its organization (workflows, permissions) and technical side. The modeling of the business objects' lifecycles is also present. Consequently, the semantic aspect does not describe the knowledge in a uniquely static manner; it also integrates a dynamic representation, in the form of the lifecycle of business objects.

With regards to the MDM system, the semantic aspect tackles the modeling of reference and master data, in the form of business objects. The lifecycles of these objects are modeled with the help of states machines. Two types of operations can be distinguished:

– *elementary business operations* correspond to the business rules that do not depend on business objects' states;

– *extended business operations*, under the control of the lifecycles of business objects, that therefore depend on the states of business objects.

The design and implementation approach of these two types of operation within the MDM system are not identical. We will return, in the following chapter, to these differences.

8.2.1.2. *Pragmatic aspect*

Definition: pragmatic aspect

The pragmatic aspect takes control of the modeling of the organization in the form of use cases (interaction of an actor with the system) and the processes or worklows (interaction between the actors). The pragmatic aspect equally describes information that concerns the organization, like, for example, the data necessary for the permissions management of IT systems, the archiving of files, the printing systems, etc.

With regards to the MDM system, the pragmatic aspect deals with the reference and master data modeling used in the organization. These are the administrative objects, similar to business objects, but situated at an organizational level.

The pragmatic aspect also provides use cases for the query and update of data, as well as organizational processes. The use cases express the organizational constraints, particularly permissions management. The processes form data approval workflows.

8.2.1.3. *Geographical aspect*

Definition: geographical aspect

The geographical aspect enables the modeling of the company structure from the point of view of its physical locations, for instance via geographical sectors such as territories, regions, countries, etc.

Applied to the MDM approach, this modeling enables the identification of geographical contexts. Each reference and master data can then be initialized and updated differently depending on the context: the name of a product is different depending on the language of the geographical sector in which it is commercially available; a promotion rate is adjusted depending on the region, etc. In practice, there are often multiple contexts which can change depending on the evolution of the company's geography and its environment.

The contexts do not only concern the geographical aspects. They are situated in a much larger management that embraces, for instance, multi-channels and organizations.

Therefore, a call center, a website, as subsidiary, or even a partner is each similar to a use context. With an MDM system, the initialization and update of the same piece of data can be different depending on these contexts. The addition of a new use context must not necessitate data modeling.

In other words, the data model is established without information about the use contexts; the geographical and pragmatic aspects are an aid to identify them but do not influence the way the business objects (semantic) and administrative objects (pragmatic) are designed.

8.2.1.4. *Logical aspect*

Definition: logical aspect

The logical aspect takes control of the upstream model derivation (semantic, pragmatic and geographical) in the form of logical models that integrate the principles of logical architecture of data and processing, like, for example, the loose coupling concept. The logical aspect is done in an architectural style which is decided before starting the derivation. On the processing side, the most common style is that of Service Oriented Architecture (SOA) to the detriment of other styles, such as the modular approach or the strictly object oriented approach. On the data side, a relational oriented approach imposes itself most of the time, which leads to the design of a "Logical Data Model" (LDM) in a relational style.

The logical models are independent of technical choices. They are re-usable throughout the evolution of technical environments (programming languages, operating systems, RDBMS, etc.).

Applied to the MDM approach, the logical aspect is primarily concerned with the architecture of data. The aim is to obtain a Logical Data Model (LDM) in terms comprehensible to the MDM software.

Logical modeling is carried out in several possible architecture styles, depending on the MDM tool chosen. Three architecture styles can be distinguished:

– the first is the most classic; this approach is in accordance with the Relational Database Management System (RDBMS). It follows classic implementation in database tools such as in DB2, Oracle, SQL-Server, etc.;

– the second is object-oriented in inspiration, with the use of an Object Oriented Database System or strictly based on XML use. The loss of the benefits of the relational approach and the differences with object orientation and the hierarchical XML approach do not enable us to profit from all these architecture styles in the same data model;

– the third architecture style brings together the relational, the object and the benefits of XML schemas, all at the same time. This results in a "semantic" logical data architecture style that uses the multi-evaluated attributes of foreign keys, mixing together the relational approach and the object oriented approach, but which also allows the attachment of rules (facets, data triggers) and nested data types (Russian doll).

The implementation of a logical data model in semantic architecture style requires the use of an MDM tool capable of supporting such a model.

In the modeling procedures describe in this book, we will concern ourselves with this type of MDM, which is able to support the Model-driven approach, in other words rich data models. To obtain an automatic alignment of the data governance functions with the models, without developing specific software, rich data models must be at hand which can unify the quality of the repository via the referential integrity constraints mechanism of the relational oriented approach, the flexibility and the expressivity of the object oriented approach and the power of the procedural attachment of data (facets, data triggers). This type of representation is available, at the software level, thanks to the use of XML schema standards. This then replaces the classic relational Data Description Language (DDL)[5].

---

5. Data Description Language. The most classic DDL is that of the description of tables in SQL (Create Table, Alter Table, Create Index, etc.). A relational DDL remains unavoidable for transactional systems (On Line

On the processing side, the logical modeling is simpler to carry out as it does not involve modeling a full OLTP system (Online Transaction Processing). The processing ensured by the MDM system is focused on the management of data integrity and their validation. They do not integrate management rules applied to transactional data.

This modeling will also enable us to introduce the SOA style by deriving the business operations (semantic models) and use cases (pragmatic models) in the form of services.

8.2.1.5. *Technical aspect*

Definition: technical aspect

This aspect describes the technical platform on which the system runs. In it is the design of the execution framework for the SOA services (e.g. spring and struts frameworks in the Java world), message exchange patterns (MEP) applied to the integration of systems[6] (synchronous, asynchronous, batch, exactly-one, at least one, etc.), IT components available such as workflow, the rules engine, etc.

The technical aspect fixes the choice of the MDM tool and the other components necessary for its integration in the Information System, in particular the message exchange patterns (MEP) for the integration of the data repository with the rest of the IT systems, the data quality tools, the

---

Transaction Processing, or OLTP) that require management of a high volume of data, with highly constrained response times. By contrast, for the requirements of reference and master data, the semantic approach is better and more cost-effective as it enables a Model-driven MDM system to be implemented. Such an MDM system ensures an optimized management of the data governance functions, and access to data repositories, without limit for the volumes and response times necessary for the management of reference and master data.

6. EAI, ESB, ETL.

use of a Business Rules Management System, the use of a workflow engine, etc.

8.2.1.6. *Software aspect*

Definition: software aspect

The software aspect corresponds to the design of the software. It relies on the technical solutions retained for software development, for example the programming languages, the use of web services, EJB, XML, etc.

In the MDM approach, the software aspect is the translation of the logical data model in a physical data schema, either of a relational DDL, or a XML schema.

The software model provides a translation of the logical model in executable terms by the MDM software tool. For instance, elementary business operations are directly generated in trigger form in pre- and post-conditions of the data update actions, following an adapted grammar and conforming to the XML schema[7] standard.

Elementary operations (CRUD[8] actions) overload the behavior, by default, of the MDM system. The extended business operations profit from either a decision table, to know the constraints brought about by the states of the business objects, or by transitions described in the lifecycle of business objects. We will return in detail to these devices in the next chapter.

The part of logical modeling that described the use cases and the processes is also part of a derivation in the software

---

7. The XML schema standard accepts being extended, which enables the MDM tool to add its own directives for data validation, for example the declaration of business rules to execute pre- and post-conditions of data updates.
8. CRUD: Create – Read – Update – Delete.

model. The use cases are translated, most commonly by access rights at the MDM system level; the processes are translated in a workflow, whether integrated in the MDM tool, or independent.

8.2.1.7. *Hardware and physical aspects*

Definition: hardware and physical aspects

The hardware and physical aspects serve to describe the hardware infrastructure and software installation. The IT production teams are generally in charge of these aspects.

In the MDM approach, we describe the physical implementation of the data repository on the IT infrastructures, particularly if a duplication of the repository exists for performance, reliability and security purposes. It is also necessary to detail the configurations of the production servers that house the MDM system, the network connections used for access, the configuration of work stations, etc.

8.2.2. *Choosing another method*

We have just described the principles of the Praxeme method, and its use in relation to the MDM approach. This capacity to customize the method to constrain and enrich it to a smaller application field, here the MDM system, is a determining factor. Indeed, a company concerned with industrializing its IS and IT work practices, must not accept the use of different methods depending on the types of projects that must be carried out.

The same modeling procedures must be used for projects involving transactional data as well as for the MDM system, even if simplification and adaptation of certain of these is necessary.

This is the case with Praxeme applied to an MDM system. In particular, the design of processes is simplified as it involves treating reference and master data approval processes in a less complex way than the processes that act on transactional data.

However, data modeling fully benefits from the force of the semantic modeling procedures offered by Praxeme. This modeling guides the construction of the data model necessary to the MDM system and favors its reuse at the time of transactional data modeling. The same business objects and lifecycles are reused to build the MDM system, to synchronize it with the rest of the IT system but also to progressively overhaul the transactions beyond the scope of the initial MDM system itself.

Consequently, a company must avoid the implementation of a method that would need to be invented just for the MDM approach. On the contrary, it is necessary that the method be based on an enterprise method and be useable across the scope of MDM requirements.

If the Praxeme method is not used, it is necessary to verify that the method envisaged to be used answers the following demands:

– there is a distinction between business modeling and modeling of organizational processes. The business modeling provides the lifecycle of the business objects, from a strictly business point of view, outside the constraints of the organization. The business objects and their lifecycles are not modeled for the sole use of the MDM system. They must be reused in order to manage the integration of the MDM system with the rest of the IT system, but also at the time of the progressive overhaul of the transactional systems. In other words, the MDM system and the transactional systems share the same data modeling;

– there is a distinction between upstream modeling (business, organization) and logical modeling;

– that it takes into consideration a logical modeling of data that reconciles simultaneously the relational approach, object oriented approach, as well as a hierarchical approach and procedural attachment (XML, facets, attachment of services to the data via pre- and post-conditions); put differently, the method must be capable of profitting from the Model-driven MDM tool and rich data models.

If these principles are respected by the method, then the modeling procedures described in this book remain valid.

8.3. The components of Enterprise Data Architecture

Once the methodological framework is set, it is possible to begin the description of semantic modeling by making clear its components, made up of business objects, of data categories and domains of business objects. These components serve to build the Enterprise Data Architecture.

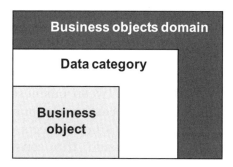

Figure 8.2. *Components of Enterprise Data Architecture*

8.3.1. *The business object*

The business object concept has been known for a number of years in the IT field but has not been used across the whole of a company's Information Systems. It only takes a few examples of business objects to understand their scope: client, citizen, organization, product, real estate inventory, payment types, etc.

The concept embodies a perception that is not one of functions nor organizational processes of a company (workflows); neither is it a technical perception such as the object oriented approach used in software engineering, organizing the real world around a large number of small data entities and processing.

Business objects are comprehensible to business users, even though these don't always perceive them as entities in their own right; they perceive them more as information flows manipulated through organizational processes.

The lack of use of the business object concept can be explained in the following manner:

– from the start of the construction of IT systems, the modular approach has had the edge over the object oriented approach. Straightaway, business objects were duplicated in silos oriented around the functions of the company;

– the way in which relational databases have been used has not left enough room for business objects. The optimization of the access to databases is done following a calibration surrounding functions within silos, rarely around business objects. This aspect changes progressively under the impulse of the Service Oriented Architecture (SOA) which organizes access to data around business objects in order to raise the reuse capacity;

– object oriented design, when it is badly carried out, handles only small dimensional objects, with very high coupling, which dilutes business objects into poorly structured class diagrams.

The MDM approach cannot afford another failure concerning the use of business objects. The rationalization of the management of reference and master data and the sharing of a common information model, across the whole company, imposes the practice of business objects shared throughout the company. Semantic modeling gives us the necessary procedures for the reactivation of the business objects concept.

First of all, semantic modeling brings together all the data in the form of semantic classes. As previously stated, these classes describe the business in an organization-independent manner. Next, a business object is a semantic class, the modeling of which is associated with a state machine that determines its lifecycle. A business object is associated with other semantic classes, some of which also have a state machine. A business object is described by a single state machine. The business objects are regrouped in the form of data categories, the properties of which are discussed in the next section.

A semantic class is modeled in the following manner:

– by its business identifier;

– by the data that it has fixed at the time of the creation of the object (header);

– by its data than can be modified after the creation of the object (body);

– by its associations with other semantic classes;

– by its elementary business operations; that is to say the operations that do not depend on the business states;

– if the semantic class has a state machine then it enriches itself with extended business operations, the execution of which is conditioned by the management of its states; it is then a business object. A decision table indicates the authorizations of data updates depending on the business object's states.

8.3.2. *The data category*

The semantic classes are regrouped around business subjects of the highest level, enabling improved understandability and the progressive design of the semantic model.

For instance, it is useful to assemble, for the same subject, the "Address" business object and all its peripheral classes such as "Postcode", "Post office", "Country", etc., at the same time. This subject then represents a data category: in this example, it is the "Geography" category.

This concept has its roots in the "Class Category" principle defined by Grady Booch [BOO 94], co-author of the UML standard. A category has a strong semantic cohesion. In particular, a category cannot contain isolated classes or several aggregates disjointed from classes. Every semantic class is filed in one and only one data category, across the whole Information System.

The data category enables a better understanding of large business subjects.

With regard to logical modeling, we will see how to use the data category in order to guarantee a loose coupling of data, i.e. limiting the overlaps of data structures (see Chapter 10).

8.3.3. *Business object domains*

The last stage of the Enterprise Data Architecture, business object domains, regroups data categories and consequently semantic classes. On average, it is enough to have less than about ten business object domains to represent the entire company.

For instance, we can identify a *"Reality"* domain that brings together business objects from the real world, such as client, third parties, club, association, address, country, vehicle, etc., themselves grouped in "geography", "intangible asset" and "person" data categories.

8.3.4. *Data repository architecture*

Without the Enterprise Data Architecture that we are describing, it would be difficult to counter the data duplication risks that could appear as early on as in data modeling. For instance, when an "employee" is modeled, how do you ensure that you do not model certain subjects that are attached to him/her? If the "geography" data category is properly identified and isolated from the rest of the models, it can be reused as a semantic concept to link employees with their addresses. On the other hand, if the semantic modeling of the address is diluted in several other models, such as those that represent real estate assets or third parties, the reusing of the address model becomes more hazardous.

The damage of data duplication in the semantic modeling are considerable, going as far as generating silo data repositories, which we are looking to avoid at all cost in the MDM approach.

These components (business objects, data categories, domains) structure the administration of reference and master data. The MDM tool presents users with the domains list, followed by the data categories within each of these domains in order to finally access the instances of the business and administrative objects[9]. This structure forms the backbone of the MDM system.

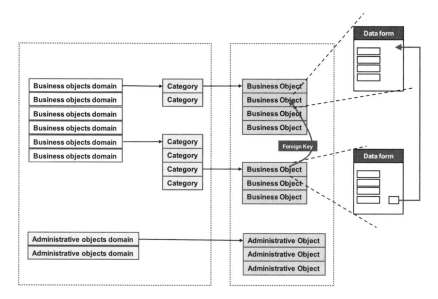

Figure 8.3. *Architecture by domains, data categories, business objects (and administrative objects)*

The MDM system users may want to manage data by functional domains that regroup business objects coming from several business domains.

To meet this requirement, the MDM system must allow the creation of data access filters that mask the foundation in business object domains, without calling it into question. The foundation must be conserved as it guarantees that there is no duplication in the data models.

---

9. The administrative objects are described in the pragmatic modeling, following identical modeling procedures to those used for business objects (Chapter 11).

8.4. The drawbacks of semantic modeling

Every modeling attempt is face with three drawbacks: a lack of return on investment, a lack of competency and the blank page effect. This also concerns the semantic modeling required by the MDM approach.

8.4.1. *The lack of return on investment*

We have already had the opportunity to present the conditions necessary to successfully transform models on return on investment (see Chapter 4). The important elements that we must bear in mind are repeated here:

– the reference and master data models are exploited by a Model-driven MDM system in order to automatically deliver the data governance functions. From this stage on, the return on investment of modeling is considerable as the business users have a data governance tool at their disposal directly aligned with the reference and master data models;

– these same data models become the canonical format of data flows in the EAI, ESB or ETL. Different to a pivot format often too rigid and technical, this canonical format expresses all the business knowledge of the data and can take variations in behavior into consideration, for instance in the data cardinality of associations[10].The streamlining of

---

10. This canonical format, in an XML schema, enriches the default management of the data cardinalities minOccurs and maxOccurs, the values of which are fixed and frozen in the description of data structures. Indeed, they are themselves managed as reference data, with values that depend on the use contexts of the canonical format. It means that the description of data structures made in the XML Schema is contextualized depending on the consumers. This is the same as extending the XML schema, which is authorized by the standard, in order to add predicates, for example in xPath, to retrieve the values minOccurs and maxOccurs depending on the use contexts. A Model-driven MDM tool is capable of implementing this type of agility on the data (see the MDM tool of Orchestra Networks for more details).

data flows as well as the improvement of their quality and reliability are important vectors of financial gains;

– these data models serve as a base for the use of the business rules management system and the actions of the overhaul of the IT system[11].

Therefore, we have at our disposal several criteria to measure the return on modeling efforts.

Other criteria exist, such as better management of the sharing and maintenance of knowledge, thanks to the availability of models.

8.4.2. *Lack of competency*

There is no easy answer to the drawbacks caused by the lack of competency in modeling. It is necessary to train actors in modeling and anticipate the need for experts to accompany the process, at least for the first few projects. Due to the fact that the modeling required for the MDM approach concerns the scope of reference and master data, the modeling procedures are taken charge of quite quickly.

Choosing to use a Model-driven MDM system, favorable to the automatic generation of screens from data models, is important in order to favor a project management by successive adjustments of the models: the modeler has data visualization tools at his disposal, which constitute a considerable aid to refine and stabilize the modeling. Model-driven MDM avoids the tunnel effect of purely theoretical modeling that would strongly increase the risk of failure. That risk is even greater when the actors do not have much practice in modeling data.

---

11. This is the *Agility Chain Management System* (ACMS) concept, already described in the first part of this book.

8.4.3. *The blank page effect*

To counter the blank page effect, the data analyst should be given a pre-built data model, ready for use, serving him as a base for his modeling work. Moreover, the blank page effect is often a negative factor when it is necessary to start a negotiation with multiple actors on data modeling that must be shared. If this negotiation starts as a blank page, without any prior proposal recognized as being acceptable or desirable, then the negotiation can be long and delicate. Also, it is best to avoid the temptation of re-engineering an existing database in order to obtain a first data model.

This approach is often destined for failure as what is already in place contains too many errors and useless complexities collected over time.

The objective of semantic modeling is to offload, once and for all, the technical and legacy constraints in order to re-appropriate business fundamentals.

To counter the blank page effect, it is necessary to use data models that are ready to use, called "patterns". Unlike other technical patterns already known to software development, such as "Factory", "Facade" or "Singleton", these are semantic modeling patterns.

8.5. Ready-to-use semantic models

Before reviewing possible reusable data model sources, it is necessary to specify that we are looking for a lot more than data models described in technical terms. We need true semantic models expressed with standard UML notation, without data duplication. These models must not be cluttered with join tables which involve a technical complication that we do not need.

These reusable semantic data models must also contain a description of the business objects' lifecycles. This last point will let us down. At best, data models with a good description of business objects exist from a static point of view, but their lifecycles are rarely available.

We will now concern ourselves with the possible principal sources of acquiring data models: software packages, industry specific models, and generic models.

8.5.1. *Software packages*

The first source of data models is brought by software packages (ERP, CRM, Supply Chain, etc.). With the acquisition of a software package, a data model should be provided. Unfortunately, software packages do not offer sufficient transparency in terms of publication of their data models.

Only technical documentation exists. Business representations are weak and rarely expressed in a UML notation.

Today, with the classic approach of software packages, semantic modeling is too often aborted from the start. A company finds itself trapped in its software package which anchors itself in the Information System like a new silo. In order for this situation to change, the software package vendors must be interested in an approach surrounding business repositories (MDM, BRMS and BPM) and publish semantic models of their reference and master data, followed by business rules. We have already discussed this new vision, in a previous chapter (see Chapter 3). Moreover, software package suffers from the same problems as do "industry specific models" that we will now describe, especially in terms of complexity which is a consequence of a weakness in Enterprise Architecture applied to the data.

8.5.2. *Industry specific models*

Several organizations sell or deliver open source data models by activity sector. We cannot cite here all these initiatives as there are many of them and they concern all activity sectors, for example:

– Telecoms: Shared Information Data model (SID) of the TMForum;

– Insurance: Association for Cooperative Operations Research and Development (ACORD);

– Finance: Financial Markup Language (FPML);

– Healthcare: Health Level Seven (HL7).

Other modeling initiatives are more generic, like, for example, the *Open Application Group, Inc.* (OAGi) but also the *Organization for the Advancement of Structured Information Standards* (OASIS). Unfortunately, all these approaches share weak points that distance them from our research into semantic models.

They have all, at least, one of the following defects:

– the data model originates from work that is focused on the standardization of data flows exchange between companies (i.e. business to business (B2B)). The models too often contain data duplications, especially in the form of information trapped in flat objects, which masks the existence of more precise objects and limits the capacity to take data validation and integrity rules into consideration;

– the data model is hyper-specialized by activity sector, such as telecommunications, banking, healthcare, etc. Consequently, the terminology used and the concepts handled are directly affected by the industry that describes them. It is impossible to understand the models without being a specialist of the relevant industry. Using such models does not answer our need to initiate the construction of one's own semantic model. These models are burdensome to a company and the effort that is made to agree to take them on board is considerable. Furthermore, they generally only cover one portion of the necessary data and their extensibility is not always evident;

– the data model is expressed is technical terms, in the form of an XML schema, or possibly a relational type, old generation DDL. Business aspect modeling in UML does not exist, or has been disintegrated. It is then difficult to understand all the richness of the handled data;

– the data model lacks a global architecture. It is rare to benefit from a normalized model in the form of components such as those which we have previously described, i.e. business object domains, data categories and business objects. There is too often a class imbroglio, with no imprint, despite this being necessary, for a Enterprise Data Architecture across the whole of the Information System.

8.5.3. *Generic data models*

These models are less ambitious than those specialized by industry. They have the advantage of being taken care of rapidly and usefully contribute to the construction of its own semantic model. These models are often more respective of an Enterprise Architecture approach, with a real concern of reusable semantic patterns.

These patterns highlight the boundaries that isolate groups of data enabling a construction by stages of its data model, following a LEGO approach. These models bring an interesting approach to counter the blank page effect of the first semantic model.

Nonetheless, initiatives for the construction and publication of such semantic patterns are rare. We will give the three most obvious: Martin Fowler, Len Silverston, and the MDM Alliance Group.

8.5.3.1. *Martin Fowler*

Martin Fowler was one of the first to work on the idea of the analysis pattern, by proposing reusable UML models to describe organizations, charts of accounts, concepts related to time management, etc., in a standardized manner. His book *Analysis Patterns: Reusable Object Models* [FOW 96], published more than ten years ago, is still remarkably relevant.

However, it seems that the Fowler's work is more oriented towards the domain of software engineering: maintaining a full quality business model level is abandoned whereas it is mandatory to counter the blank page effect at the start of semantic modeling.

8.5.3.2. *Len Silverston*

Len Silverston has written several books dedicated to the presentation of reusable data models, the vocation of which is universal, beyond a particular industrial sector. His book, *"The Data Model Resource Book – Volume 1"* [SIL 01] is a mine of information that presents, in a progressive manner, a great many business domains (justifying modeling choices, benefits and constraints) such as "person", "organization", "product", "order", "delivery", "billing", "human resources", etc.

However, the Silverston's models are provided in terms comprehensible only by IT practitioners. It is close to the logical data model, which takes us away from semantic modeling. In particular, join tables are apparent, the lifecycles on the business objects do not exist and the

Enterprise Architecture, by business object domains, data categories and business objects, is not easy to spot.

8.5.3.3. *MDM Alliance Group (MAG)*

Unlike earlier initiatives, the ready-to-use models made available by the MDM Alliance Group, have been taken up by the community. This is not work based on the isolated creation of an individual. Several actors intervened to establish and bring these data models to life[12].

This initiative, launched in 2008, still has some way to go before achieving a sufficient maturity level, but the main principles are defined around key concepts such as the modeling of "party", "asset", "real estate", "address", "contact", "event", "classification", "concepts related to time management", "human resources", etc.

The models delivered by the MDM Alliance Group conform to the requirements of semantic modeling. They use the UML notation in business terms, with no useless technical representation. These models are built in an Enterprise Architecture that is based on business object domains, data categories and business objects.

In the following chapter, we will present a few examples of these models, which will enable us to describe, in more detail, the procedures of semantic modeling.

---

12. In particular, Dominique Vauquier (expert on semantic modeling and author of the Praxeme method) and Pierre Bonnet (founder of the MDM Alliance Group).

Chapter 9

Semantic Modeling Procedures

In the previous chapter, we set the scene for semantic modeling. We will now describe the detailed procedures for this modeling, basing ourselves on a case study. The data models used in this chapter are taken, unless otherwise stated, from documents from the MDM Alliance Group (MAG)[1]. All models respect the UML standard notation. These procedures benefit from the Praxeme method, made available free of charge by the Praxeme Institute. The semantic modeling procedures form a tool box destined for business users as well as for the IT department. The organization required to profit from this has already been discussed in Chapter 7.

9.1. A practical case of semantic modeling: the address

To facilitate our understanding of the process of semantic modeling, let us take a practical case: formatting of addresses. The business object "address" is sufficiently universal to avoid a functional description phase. This object is also sufficiently complex, notably when addresses have to

---

1. http://www.mdmalliancegroup.com

be presented in an international manner, to allow us to have a 360° view of the modeling approach.

For pedagogical purposes, we are firstly going to examine a data model which does not respect the objectives of semantic modeling, although this model is based on UML notation and is suggested by a standards setting body.

9.1.1. Non-compliant version of semantic modeling

Figure 9.1 presents the address data model suggested by OASIS, a well-known standards setting body[2].

We notice many functional dependency links of the data straight away. For example, there are relationships which are not represented between department ("Department"), the name of the town ("CityName") or the postal zone ("PostalZone"). As this information is collected directly in the address class ("Address"), it is impossible to formally express the referential integrity constraints which exist between them. The data model is therefore impoverished; it is not a semantic data model for it lacks an element which relates to the rules of integrity.

This functional dependency link leads to the maintenance of duplication of data since, for example, the name of the town ("CityName") is duplicated as many times as the address. If the name of the town needed to be modified, we cannot see how the updating of the addresses in this town could be processed efficiently.

Unfortunately, our first conclusions about this modeling will not always be identified as problems in the application it is used for. It is likely that the objective of this modeling is to rationalize data flows between systems. We therefore have a

---

2. Address model extract from OASIS' Universal Business Language 1.0; see http://docs.oasis-open.org/ubl/cd-UBL-1.0/

very basic modeling of the address; a sort of flat file structure which is only valid for the transport of information. In this case, we could question the reasons why the modeler decided to represent countries ("Country") in the form of an entire class, no doubt in order to avoid functional dependency links and data overlap. This principle seems only to have been adopted to represent countries, which is not homogeneous with the rest of the modeling.

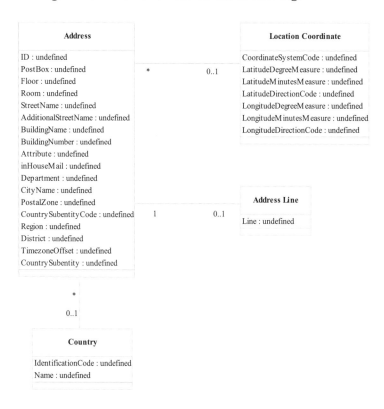

Figure 9.1. *Address modeled in a non-semantic manner (source: OASIS)*

In reality, even this attempt at a justification of the model, on the pretext of its limited use in the exchange of information between systems, is not acceptable. Indeed, in the first chapter of this book, we saw how each datum duplicated between the systems is subject to governance by the MDM solution; we have also explained that this concerns the exchange of data between companies. The MDM system ensures the traceability of these exchanges and verifies the integrity of the information before making it available to other systems. To achieve this, the MDM system must automatically enforce referential integrity constraints through data modeling. If the data model is impoverished, as in this first version of the address model, the MDM system has no jurisdiction. So then, bespoke and hard-coded software must, at EAI-ESB level, be developed in order to analyze the data flows, and strictly enforce the rules for validation.

The more impoverished the data model is, the more bespoke software development is necessary to restore the integrity of the data. This design is expensive and locks business knowledge in hard-coded software. The objective of semantic modeling is to restore power to the data model in order to reduce the need for this type of design.

With an address model of this type, it is impossible to ensure a real traceability of data flows exchanged between systems. By memorizing the addresses with the help of this model, we can obtain a technical audit trail of data flows only, since the relationships between the data are not fully expressed. It is thus complex to execute data queries of the type "get a list of all the addresses exchanged with a company whose town is in a given country". The solution necessitates a lookup of the totality of the addresses because there is no relationship between countries ("Country") and cities ("CityName").

To complete the critical analysis of this first version of the model, we must also take note of the absence of names of the associations. In this data model, quite short, it is easy to guess the meaning of the associations; this is no longer acceptable when the model is extended. We must also point out that the names of the datum are not formulated in semantic level terms. There is already a logical codification which needlessly penalizes the reading of the model by business users.

9.1.2. *First draft of semantic modeling*

The following model (Figure 9.2) is a first start at a semantic modeling of the address. Unlike the previous model, we have deleted all the functional dependency links between data. The effect of this is that information on countries, towns, post offices and postal codes no longer appears in the class "Address". It is expressed in the form of associations towards other classes. We will see this part of the modeling later in this section.

We establish that the address is now attached to a "Site" enabling us to specify a different formulation according to the language used.

This situation can occur in regions which use several languages for the same address. Other utilizations can be envisaged, such as the formulation of the address in an electronic language which is different to that known today in postal systems. Thus, unlike the previous model, we can anticipate the inclusion of many types of geo-localization systems (GPS, Galileo, etc.).

The address, throughout the Site, is attached to an Object and a Period of validity. The former is a generalization of objects declared elsewhere in the model, such as Organizations, Third Parties, Apartment buildings, Tangible assets, etc. The qualifier attribute "Location nature" allows us to define the type of utilization of the address: usual, professional, personal, second home, invoicing, return

(return address in case of problem with the product), vacations, etc.

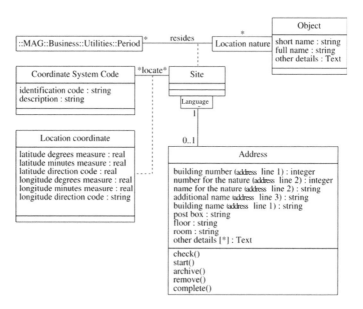

Figure 9.2. *Semantic modeling of the Address*
(first part, source: MAG)

We are progressively discovering the semantics of the address but so far it still remains a static perspective. Now we have to concern ourselves with the business lifecycle of the address.

9.1.3. *Modeling of the lifecycle of the address*

Semantic modeling must express everything about the address. It must not be confined to a static description. We also have to model it's dynamics from a business point of view, which allows us to assert the data validation rules depending on the address's states. Figure 9.3 shows the final result of this dynamic modeling, in the form of a state machine in UML. These address states are not dependent on the organization of the company; they only express the core business, that is to say, the semantics, of the address.

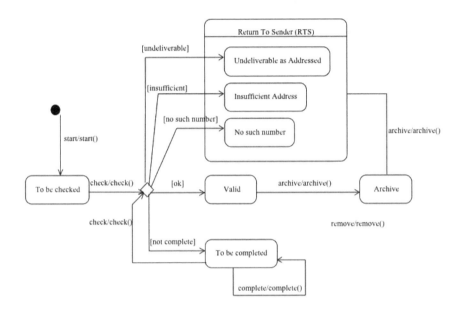

Figure 9.3. *The Address's business lifecycle (source: MAG)*

This UML model is simple to read, providing that the principles of its notation have already been mastered.

For example, when the address is in the business state "To be checked", it is possible to trigger an operation of verification of the address "check/check ()" which determines the quality of the address and consequently assigns it a business state. The address then switches to the state "valid", "to be completed", or "Return To Sender (RTS)" with a substate making it possible to define in detail the cause of the RTS: "Undeliverable", "Insufficient Address" or "No such number".

The reading of the rest of the model follows this same principle of notation. When a transition between two states holds an expression of the type "check/check ()", it means that the first part of this expression "check" corresponds to the intention to carry out the verification operation; it is an event.

The second part of the expression "check ()" corresponds to the actual execution of the verification operation as soon as the event has been accepted by the state machine, that is to say that the current state of the address is, in this example, either "To be checked", or "To be completed".

As a result of this modeling work, we can identify business operations which allow the transition from one business state to another; in our example, the following operations take place, which we can easily identify through transitions between states: "start()", "check()", "complete()", "archive()", "remove()".

These operations are naturally attached to the class "Address" (see following figure). The operations "start()" and "remove()" allow the state machine to be activated the moment a new address is created, and to delete it at the time that the address is definitively deleted, once the time limit for data archiving has expired.

The UML state machine enables the rich and varied lifecycle of data to be designed. Our objective here is not to go into a detailed account of the power of this notation. The state machine which we have described for the address only utilizes a small part of the possibilities offered by the UML notation. It must be understood that modeling with state machines is necessary so that the MDM system can fully guarantee the integrity of data on three levels: data validation, states validation and transitions execution. We will now detail the role of each of these levels.

Address
building number (address line 1): integer number for the nature (address line 2): integer name for the nature (address line 2): string additional name (address line 3): string building name (address line 1): string post box: string floor: string room: string other details [*]: text
check() start() archive() removed() completed()

Figure 9.4. *The semantic class with its extended business operations (source: MAG)*

9.1.3.1. *Data validation*

On the basis of the state machine, we can establish a decision table which specifies, for each datum of the address, whether it is possible to modify it or not according to the current state of the address (Figure 9.5).

ADDRESS	BUSINESS STATES							
	To be checked	Valid	To be completed	Return to Sender (RTS)	Undeliverable as Addressed	Insufficient Address	No such number	Archive
building number	yes	no	yes	no	no	no	no	no
number for the nature	yes	no	yes	no	no	no	no	no
name for the nature	yes	no	yes	no	no	no	no	no
additional name	yes	no	yes	no	no	no	no	no
building name	yes	no	yes	no	no	no	no	no
post box	yes	no	yes	no	no	no	no	no
floor	yes	no	yes	no	no	no	no	no
room	yes	no	yes	no	no	no	no	no
other details[*]	yes	yes	yes	yes	yes	yes	yes	no

yes = modification possible / no = modification impossible

Figure 9.5. *The decision table for the modification of the address (source: MAG)*

Before making any attempt to modify a datum of the address, the MDM system automatically consults this decision table in order to determine whether or not it is possible, taking into account the current state value of the address, to allow this modification.

This decision table is in itself master data governed by the MDM system. It can therefore be subject to different initializations and updates according to the use contexts (head office, subsidiary, partner, country etc.) and versions. Rather than hard-coding these rules and taking the risk of delivering too rigid and heavy a bespoke software, it is more judicious to put this decision table in place, and customizing the MDM system by a simple setting of values within those tables.

The state RTS ("Return To Sender") is a super state which encompasses the three sub-states "Undeliverable as Addressed", "Insufficient Address" and "No such number". By default, the sub-states inherit a set value from their super state, which is the case in this example[3]. It would still be possible to envisage that the datum "building number" can be modified when the sub-state value is "No such number". In this case, the state machine should anticipate the possibility of re-checking an address which has fallen into RTS, which is not possible in our current state machine.

9.1.3.2. *State validation*

The State machine also allows MDM, if we want it to take on this task, to verify that the business lifecycle of the master data "state" conforms to the specification. For example, if the address is in the state "Valid" then the only possible change of state is "Archive". All other attempts to change the state are rejected by the MDM system. Here, too, a decision table is used to control the changes of state.

---

3. The inherited data appear in italics in the decision table.

9.1.3.3. *Transition execution*

The MDM system can also take on the responsibility of triggering business operations which change the state of the address. For example, the operation "check ()" of verification of the address, can be triggered directly by the MDM system.

The MDM system then launches a tool to analyze the quality of the address, which returns a result enabling the MDM system to calculate the next state of the address. This kind of responsibility is not mandatory.

9.1.4. *Complete semantic modeling of the address*

The continuation of the modeling of the address leads us to unveil the semantic classes associated with the business object "Address".

These classes formally express the functional dependency link which were concealed in the initial version suggested by OASIS. This modeling also takes into account the requirement to be universal by proposing a data structure able to embrace the different representations of the address in different countries.

This data model, to which is added the state machine, the decision tables, and the links with "Site" and "Object" which we saw earlier, constitutes a complete semantic model of the address.

This model enables the MDM system to fully guarantee the integrity of the master data, and to do so without any superfluous software development work.

We should not be worried about the apparent complexity of the semantic model we obtain at the end. Certainly, it is more extended than the initial model, but it is a lot more powerful and thus limits bespoke software developments outside of the MDM system.

This model is not yet a description of the tables in a databases. The question of the derivation of semantic classes in a logical data model is dealt with in Chapter 11

Readers interested in a detailed explanation of this model will find the description of each semantic class and association in the Appendix at the end of this book.

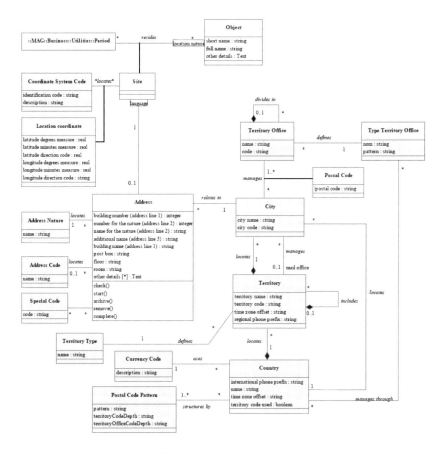

Figure 9.6. *Semantic modeling of the Address (complete version, source: MAG)*

9.2. Example of Enterprise Data Architecture

As we saw in the previous chapter, the business objects and all the semantic classes are arranged in architectural components formed by data categories, and then by business object domains[4]. Rather than start from scratch in order to build this data architecture, we can usefully draw inspiration from the one proposed by the MDM Alliance Group which we use again here. It has a level of universality which is sufficiently high to enable it to be used as a foundation for semantic modeling in most companies.

Figure 9.7 is a diagram of the packages in UML. The dotted lines represent the dependency links between the packages.

The first level of packages reveals the business object domains: "Catalog", "Reality", "Portfolio", "Service delivery", "Accounting", "Human resources", "Supervision". Inside each of these packages, we discover a first, non-exhaustive list of data categories. For example, for the package "Reality", we have the following data categories available: "Person", "Party", "Real estate", "Tangible assets", "Supply capability", and "Geography".

We find in the data category "Geography" the business object "Address" and all the semantic classes which are attached to it. In this way, the address is modeled in an independent and re-usable way. When the data analyst needs to describe the addresses, s/he combines its semantic model with the data category "Geography". Using this principle, the same representation of the address is required for all third parties and real estate assets.

---

4. "Administrative objects" also exist, similar to business objects, but designed with data related to the organizational aspects of the system (see Chapter 10).

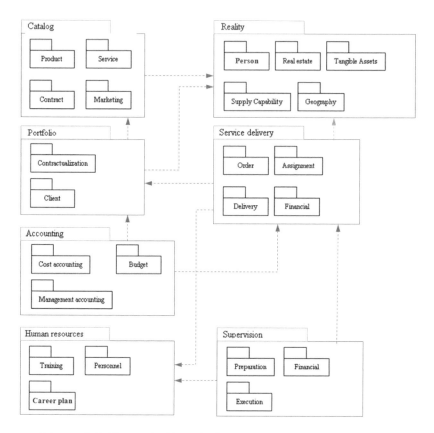

Figure 9.7. *Enterprise Data Architecture example (source: MAG)*

This re-utilization has consequences for the project management of MDM. For example, if the first data repository concerns employees, the description of the address must not be specified in the human resources field. Instead, we would favor a universal representation of the address, based on a semantic model with the power to respond to the needs of the management of addresses, beyond the scope of HR.

For example, the moment that the second data repository appears (real estate), the same semantic model of the category "Geography" must be re-used in order to counter any deviation by silos from the modeling. If semantic modeling tolerates data duplications then the penalty at the development software level is immediate and acute: the company gets MDM by silos, which leads to new problems in data quality.

To avoid overlap within the semantic models themselves, it is imperative to dispose of an Enterprise Data Architecture such as that just presented.

The utilization of this architecture means that we accept the sharing of semantic models, sharing them, using them in a LEGO approach (plug and play use of data categories) during the modeling process.

We should keep in mind two leading principles which contribute to the success of this approach:

– we have to organize the work appropriately in order to anticipate and counteract the risks implicit in mutualization. These risks are revealed when the data models evolve, since the changes impact all the actors involved in the same data representation (we have already dealt with this subject in Chapter 7 dedicated to organization);

– the data categories must be structurally isolated from each other in the software, in order to allow the LEGO construction, meaning a plug and play use of data categories. To fully achieve this, we will see that Logical Data Architecture introduces a special derivation mechanism of the data categories of the semantic model into the logical data model, in order to obtain the necessary separation of business objects. This mechanism is sufficiently strong enough to allow a change of data category without questioning the entire data model. We will see this principle in Chapter 10, which is devoted to logical architecture.

The most complete description of the Enterprise Data Architecture presented here is available directly from the MDM Alliance Group website[5].

9.3. Semantic modeling procedures

Fortified with the knowledge of the first principles of modeling, discovered through our case study of the business object "Address", we will now review the important points to retain. We will detail four types of business operations which steer the modeling and prepare the way for logical modeling; these are extended, elementary, single-occurrence, and multi-occurrence business operations. We continue by presenting principles which favor upgradeability of models, and then finish with a list of other useful procedures to take into account to leverage the data models quality.

9.3.1. *Extended business operation*

A business operation is "extended" when its execution depends on the business states of its business object.

To uncover these operations, we must first model the business object's lifecycle, in the form of state machine. The following is a reminder of the standard UML notation.

Figure 9.8. *Reminder of the UML notation for state machine*

---

5. http://www.mdmalliancegroup.com

Thanks to this state machine, we dispose of three kinds of information which enable us to design extended business operations:

– the values of the state form enumeration data for the master data "state" of the business object concerned with the state machine. These values are used at the moment that the modifications of the master data are validated; that is to say, as a pre-condition of the actions of the MDM system (decision tables);

– the state value changes only by respecting transitions described by the state machine;

– the transitions which link two states automatically cause the business operations to be revealed at the time that the state machine is being modeled.

We will now take each of these points in turn and detail the methods of application.

9.3.1.1. *Pre-condition of modification*

An extended business operation which acts as a pre-condition of the modification of the data repository, without modification of the state, does not appear in the state machine. It has no responsibility for the change of state value of the business object.

Nevertheless, this operation disposes of a pre-condition which depends on the current state value of the business object and which allows it to determine whether it is possible or not to comply. This pre-condition complies either when a screen of the MDM system is initialized[6], in order to contextualize the data input form according to the state of the business object, or at the time of data validation.

---

6. Driven by a use case which takes charge of the man–machine dialog (see Chapter 11).

The operations in charge of the creation and the deletion of a business object have an impact on the state of the object and must appear on the state machine, at least as start and end states of the machine.

Based on the states utilized by the state machine, we can define the decision table for the modification of business objects. This table describes the possibilities for updating each datum according to each business state (Figure 9.9). The MDM system automatically exploits this decision table in order to contextualize the data input screen and/or confirm the modification according to the current state value of the business object.

BUSINESS OBJECT	BUSINESS STATES			
	State 1	State 2	State 3	State 4
Data 1	yes	no	yes	no
Data 2	yes	no	yes	no
Data 3	yes	no	yes	no
Data 4	yes	no	yes	no
Data 5	yes	no	yes	no
Data 6	yes	yes	yes	yes

yes = transition authorized / no = transition forbidden

Figure 9.9. *Example of a decision table for the modification of a business object*

As we have already said, this decision table is in itself master data, which is governed by the MDM system. In this way, it can be initialized and updated differently according to the versions and uses contexts such as subsidiaries, partners, channels etc.

9.3.1.2. *Control of the change of state value*

The state is a very important master data for the integrity of the data. The enumeration of the potential values of the state of a business object and the rules governing its evolution are expressed by the state machine. We can then confer to the MDM system the responsibility for checking that the values of the state conform to the enumeration and that the changes of state respect the directives of the state machine. This responsibility does not mean that the MDM system itself modifies the value of the state of the business object. It is confined to receiving a request to modify the state, either by a human actor through a user interface, or via a system.

BUSINESS STATE – FROM	BUSINESS STATE – TO					
	Start	State 1	State 2	State 3	State 4	End
Start		yes				
State 1			yes	yes		
State 2					yes	yes
State 3					yes	yes
State 4						yes
End						

yes = transition authorized / no = transition forbidden

Figure 9.10. *Example of a decision table to monitor a change of state values*

This decision table is the outcome of the translation of the state machine given in Figure 9.11.

To put this control in place, we merely have to establish a decision table which covers the possibilities of transitions between the states, which are already expressed by the state machine. As a pre-condition of the modification of the master data "State", the MDM system automatically exploits this decision table to monitor the integrity of the requested modification. This decision table corresponds to the state machine (simplified notation) presented in Figure 9.11.

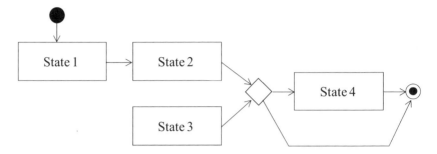

Figure 9.11. *State machine of the preceding decision table (simplified notation)*

9.3.1.3. *Execution of the transition*

In this case, the MDM system has the responsibility for triggering the execution of the business operations which appear during the transitions between states. These operations are very important as they act directly on the state values of the business object.

It is not always easy to confer a responsibility of this nature to the MDM system. The decision to trigger a change of state value in a business object should remain the prerogative of the transactional systems. As we saw in the previous section, that does not prevent the MDM system from being able to guarantee the control of the changes of states.

Nevertheless if we decide to situate the execution of the transitions directly in the MDM system, that means that the data repository has to be equipped with an state machine execution engine, that is to say, with a BPM in order to avoid a hard-coded software development.

9.3.1.4. *Synthesis*

Extended business operations must be modeled with care, for their interactions with the business object states are of great importance for the integrity of the MDM system. If these operations are not modeled as we have just indicated, using state machines and decision tables, then the MDM system will not be able to ensure, in an autonomous way, the integrity of the data that it claims to administer. In that case, provision for bespoke hard-coded software development has to be made, in order to implement the rules which manipulate the states. The risk of this situation is that it might lead to the paralysis of the MDM system, giving rise to a new and opaque application silo which is to be avoided at all costs.

Finally, extended business operations are put into the class of the business object in the following way:

– an operation "update()" for the operation of the pre-condition of the modification. This operation utilizes the decision table which makes it possible to individually modify the data and the state of the business object;

– an operation "checkState()" for the control of the changing of the state values. This operation utilizes the decision table which makes it possible to change the state values;

– each operation which appears upon a transition of the state machine is declared in the class of the business object.

9.3.2. *Elementary business operation*

A business operation is "elementary" when its execution does not depend on the business states of the objects. They are described independently of the business states. They don't appear in the state machines; they cannot interact with the states and do not have decision tables.

Each elementary business operation is inscribed in the class of its business object with an indication of its execution mode (trigger): before update, after update, after deletion, before deletion, etc. For example, if there is a need to modify the label of a product, an elementary business operation "AfterUpdateProduct()" is declared, which is triggered by the MDM system at the time that the update is validated. This operation can control, for example, that the update respects the rules of syntax agreed in advance: label inferior to a given number of characters, absence of certain characters, mandatory use of a particular character, etc.

In this example, if it was necessary to constrain the modification of the product's label by an advance verification of the state of the business object "Product", then an extended business operation would intervene; it would not simply be a question of an elementary business operation. More precisely, the extended business operation would, firstly, be triggered by the MDM system in order to verify that the modification of the label is possible, taking into account the current state value of the business object Product; then the execution of the elementary operation for the modification of the label would follow.

9.3.3. *Single-occurrence and multi-occurrence business operations*

A business operation is "single-occurrence" when its execution affects only a single instance of a business object. Conversely, a business operation is "multi-occurrence" when it acts on several instances of the same business object. This distinction ensures that the semantic modeling takes care of batch type operations which are too often, wrongly, forgotten in the MDM system approach. This allows software development to be attentive to the correct management of transactions, either in single or multi-occurrence mode.

For example, it is possible to plan ahead for a multi-occurrence operation which modifies all the labels of products by adding a prefix according to the year, the geographical commercial zone and the type of distribution channel. This multi-occurrence operation can be of an elementary nature, that is to say not taking into account the business state of the products. It can be an extended business operation with constraints which depend on the business states.

9.3.4. *Fostering the upgradeability of data models*

In this section, we bring together the recommendations which favor the upgradeability of the semantic model. We will not repeat the first of these which concerns the lack of data duplications. We have already seen how overlaps can be countered thanks to an Enterprise Data Architecture map which determines the components of business object domains, data categories and business objects.

9.3.4.1. *Variants of modeling*

A semantic model must be sufficiently universal to be useable in different contexts. For example, we already know that the cardinalities of the associations must not be frozen at the time of modeling. It is better to consider them as master data with initializations and modifications which are assured by the MDM system, according to the different use contexts of the data model.

In the same way, the initializations and modification of the data according to use contexts must not be formalized in the semantic model. For example, it is not obligatory to create a class "Language" to manage several languages. Indeed, the MDM tool must allow the multiple initializations and modifications of each datum value according to the use contexts; language is just a context like any other.

Nevertheless, the existence of use contexts can be modeled for documentation purposes, for example at the same time as the geographical representation of the company is set, through its territories, distribution networks, etc. In any case, since these contexts can change over time, you must not impose an update of semantic models to take into account new ones or delete others.

9.3.4.2. *Temporal scalability*

At a certain place in the model, the data analyst can provide for meta-data, which allows a list of data to be declared in the form of an information structure of the type: {name of the data, type of data[7], value of the data, period of validity, documentation of the data}. For the MDM system, this meta-data is master data like any other. Consequently, the user, if they have the authorization, can declare new data at this place in the model.

For example, for the configuration of products, the data analyst provides for "additional characteristic" meta-data which authorizes the addition of information unknown at the time of modeling. Since this new data can also be attached to a period of validity, we therefore dispose of a means of extending the model over time. In our example, we can indicate that certain characteristics will only be available as from a date in the future.

This approach, by using meta-data, remains simple and might turn out to be insufficient. Indeed, the added data is elementary. It is not possible to declare new complex information structures. In the same way, it is not possible to declare rules for the validation of this data. Other constraints can appear, in particular the management of rights of access to new data declared in this dynamic way. Finally, this usage must be reserved for specific cases of extension of models. Indeed, the data declared are no longer documented by the model itself, which reduces its quality

---

7. String, Integer, Date, etc.

and its expressiveness. To go further, two other approaches are possible: temporal inclusion and dynamic modeling.

Temporary inclusion

A data model can include another one. This inclusion can be associated with a predicate, in particular a temporal one. As long as the predicate is not valid, the initial data model is used. When the predicate is effective, at an agreed date, the inclusion of complementary data is triggered. The temporal predicate is in itself master data, the initialization of which is the responsibility of the business users.

We can, for example, couple this possibility with the management of use contexts. With this in mind, the initialization of the predicate is different according to the use context of the data model. It would then be possible to include the new part of the model at different timed stages according to whether the use context of the initial model is a subsidiary or the head office. Here the subsidiary and the head office represent two examples of different contexts.

Dynamic modeling

The MDM system tool has a governance feature which allows data to be modeled directly by authorized users, most of the time in a test environment. On condition that this modeling takes into account the timing aspect, that is to say the possible period of application of the changes made to the model, then this can be described as temporal management applied to the data model. In this case, it would remain to be seen how the MDM system deals with the management of the different versions of the models.

9.3.4.3. *Transversal domain*

To complement the business object domains, it is necessary to provide for a transversal domain, accessible from all the other domains. This domain collects re-usable semantic models on transverse themes, like, for example, time management, classifications, events, a thesaurus, etc. This domain also collects abstract types of data, like date formats, simple enumerations, etc.[8]

9.3.4.4. *Topics to be excluded from semantic modeling*

The more the semantic model concentrates on the representation of the core business, the greater its potential for upgradeability. Consequently, we should take advantage of MDM software to exclude from the model the features made available by the tool.

In particular, the following points should be noted, certain of which have already been quoted above:

– management of the versions of the data;

– initialization and modification of the data by use context;

– inheritance of values through an affiliation of use contexts; based on a default initialization of the data (the root use context), it is possible to create sub use contexts which enable values to be overloaded;

– permission management;

– traceability of data access (audit trail);

– data history management.

These functions are those of the data governance brought about by the MDM system; we can understand that semantic modeling, if it were to take this into account, would become more complex.

---

8. See the MDM *Alliance Group* site for examples of semantic models in transversal domains: http://www.mdmalliancegroup.com

9.3.5. *Other principles*

To finish this chapter, we will now bring together some complementary principles on the following themes: data enumerations, user identification, computed information and documentation of data.

9.3.5.1. *Data enumerations*

Enumerations are structures of data which rely on a simple code-label type model, without any relationships with other types of data.

At the time of the semantic modeling, we can create enumerated types in order to deposit in the models the knowledge of certain sets of values. This possibility must only concern enumerations of limited size (less than about thirty values) and without taking into account the needs for contextualization at this level (languages, versions, dates of validity, etc.). The management of the largest lists of data enumerations and their initialization by use contexts are dealt with directly by the MDM tool, outside of the computer-aided software engineering (CASE) modeling tool.

Thus, the capture of the data enumerations values in the CASE modeling tool is not advisable for the administration of this data, as it necessitates data governance functions which are not available in the modeling tools: management of the versions, initialization of the labels according to the use contexts (languages, countries, organizations, etc.), management of permissions, management of dates of validity, etc. These functions of governance are those of the MDM system.

9.3.5.2. *Identifiers*

At the semantic modeling stage, the design of object' identifiers is not obligatory. Nevertheless, if the data analyst has this information, it is useful to capitalize on it at this stage, generally in the form of a comment associated with the data which corresponds to the identifier attribute.

9.3.5.3. *Computed information*

Computed information (a UML derived attribute) is specified as soon as the semantic model is elaborated, which allows new rules to be identified, in the form of operations attached to the semantic classes.

9.3.5.4. *Data documentation*

The documentation of information is formalized from the beginning of the modeling. The UML CASE modeling should also allow the management of this documentation according to language, which is rarely the case. The relationship between the documentation and the UML models must be examined, using a multi-lingual dictionary. The ISO/CEI 11179[9] norm proposes a typical framework of the documentation of information. The utilization of a subset of this framework is generally sufficient with, for example, a short label, a long label, a date of creation and the date of the last update.

---

9. http://metadata-standards.org/11179/

Chapter 10

Logical Data Modeling

Business modeling using semantic models is conducted in terms which are comprehensible by business users (see Chapters 8 and 9). Now we must translate it into logical terms, interpretable by the MDM software. To carry out this translation, we must use derivation procedures from semantic modeling on the logical data model. This work is led by IT specialists, without the obligatory involvement of users.

10.1. The objectives of logical modeling

In the MDM field, logical modeling mainly concerns the Logical Data Model (LDM). This is established in the architectural style of the Model-driven MDM system, that is to say combining, at the same time, the relational approach, the object oriented approach and XML schema with hierarchies of types and data validation rules (XML facets).

This model supplies the logical schema for the MDM database; it is situated at the same level as a relational logical data model (RDBMS) but with a greater richness brought about by the object oriented approach and XML schema.

The logical model for processing remains simple since the MDM system simply attaches validation rules to the data. There is no software architecture which needs to be planned beyond that already acquired as a result of semantic modeling, through the domains of business objects, data categories and business objects. The style chosen to organize the processing, from a logical point of view, is that of Service Oriented Architecture (SOA); it allows us to constitute services which respect the classic properties of loose coupling, stateless execution and signature by data flow rather than with atomic parameters. These properties are not specific to the MDM system approach; they concern SOA and are not detailed here[1].

Logical modeling also concerns the derivation of organizational models, that is to say, the workflow (data approval processes) and the use cases; we will look at this aspect in the following chapter. Finally, the question of the integration of the MDM system with the rest of the IT system is dealt with in Chapter 12; we will see that it does not require specific modeling procedures but that it takes into account usual integration patterns between systems.

10.2. The components of logical data modeling

Logical modeling reutilizes the components already positioned in semantic modeling, that is to say, the domains of business objects, the data categories and the business objects. To complement these components, logical data modeling adds three more which allow the precise nature of

---

1. For more information on SOA properties see Pierre Bonnet *et al.*, *Sustainable IT Architecture: The progressive way of overhauling Information Systems with SOA*, Chapter 5 (The properties of SOA), ISTE–WILEY [BON 09].

the type of data which is handled to be defined: "simple data type", "complex data type" and "table":

– "simple data type" is formed by a single piece of information, without any nested data types. This is an elementary type of data: integer, string, date, enumerated data, etc.;

– "complex data type" is formed from several pieces of "simple" and "complex" data types and tables. "Complex data type", unlike a table, does not declare an identifier in the sense of a primary key (PK) found in the relational oriented approach;

– a "table" is a complex type of data with a primary key (PK), in the sense of the relational oriented approach. This key ensures the unique identification of each occurrence of the table.

All arrangements between the different kinds of data structure are possible, including multi-valued information. For example, we can model a table with columns formed by multi-occurrence complex data type.

Finally, the term of business operation, used in semantic modeling, is translated into a "service" at the logical modeling level, the latter being in SOA style.

10.3. The principle of loose-coupling data

The logical architect[2] decides on the internal structure of the domains of business objects issued from semantic modeling. These domains are broad, composed of several dozens of business objects, and the coupling between the

---

2. The work of the logical architect has a range of action over the whole of the information system. S/he guarantees the logical data architecture. To respect this architecture, logical designers use derivation procedures to establish logical data models and processing.

data has no boundaries. In other words, the semantic classes are linked to each other without any limits of depth, which is normal since the semantic model is a knowledge model without any coupling constraints.

On the other hand, at the logical level, the conservation of such a coupling could turn out to be catastrophic for performance at the moment of access to the database: the querying of information might lead to access to all the linked information even if it is are not asked for. To reduce this coupling, the logical architect disposes of data categories. Grady Booch, co-author of the UML standard, created the original concept of data categories or class category. The following quotation from the Geant4 organization is useful for understanding the benefits of the data category concept:

"In *Object-oriented Analysis and Design Methodology* by Grady Booch [BOO 94], class categories are used to create logical units. They are defined as "clusters of classes that are themselves cohesive, but are loosely coupled relative to other clusters." This means that a class category contains classes which have a close relationship (for example, the "has-a" relation). However, relationships between classes which belong to different class categories are weak, i.e., only limited classes of these have "uses" relations" [AMA 05].

In this way, a category generally regroups a maximum of five business objects, in strong semantic cohesion. The categories must be isolated from each other. This isolation means, from the point of view of the structures of the data, that the use of nested data types between business objects of different categories is not allowed. The categories are only known to each other, from a data structure point of view, through the keys (Primary Keys, Foreign keys). The categories are already positioned at the semantic modeling level since they are useful for organizing knowledge in the form of business topics. At logical modeling level, they are used again to organize the coupling between data (Figure 10.1).

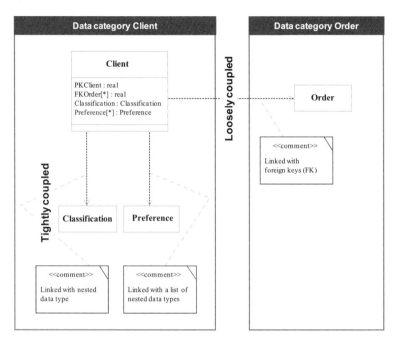

Figure 10.1. *Tight and loose data coupling*

The classes "Client", "Classification" and "Preference" are situated in the same data category: "Client"; in this situation, the intertwining of data types is possible (tight coupling). Conversely, the class "Order" is situated in another data category: "Order". The liaison between the classes "Client" and "Order" crosses two categories of data; in this case, we do not allow tight coupling of the data in order to favor the use of foreign keys, here multi-valued (loose coupling). Figure 10.2 is an example of the derivation of semantic classes in the form of three data categories: "Person", "Object" and "Geography". Each category is embodied with the help of a UML package.

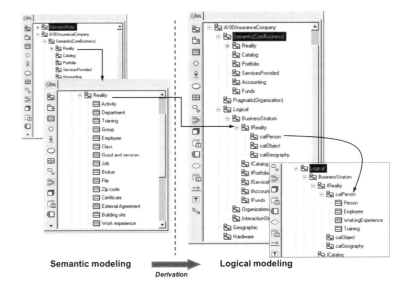

Semantic modeling ➡ **Logical modeling**

Derivation

Figure 10.2. *Example of derivation of semantic classes in data categories*

In this example, semantic modeling does not include the clustering of business objects in the form of categories; this is a possible choice of modeling which then contents itself with domains of business objects (Reality, Catalog, Portfolio, Services Provided, Accounting). In this approach, the data categories appear only in logical modeling.

The transversal domain, which collects the basic types of data (simple and complex), can also be subject to arrangement in the form of categories in order to facilitate its organization. It is not always necessary to build in categories for the administrative objects[4], as there are a smaller number of these than business objects. The administrative objects are sufficiently far away from each other from a semantic point of view to avoid the use of nested

---

4. See Chapter 11 devoted to the modeling of an organization: the administrative objects are similar to the business objects but concern information relative to the description of the organization.

types. It is more relevant to use primary and foreign keys to link administrative objects with each other. Each data category is embedded in the form of a package in UML.

10.4. The data architecture within categories

Inside data categories, the use of complex types of data rather than tables[5] is decided by the logical designer, at the time of the derivation of the semantic model. The criteria for choosing between complex data types and tables depend on the MDM software tool.

In order to illustrate the differences between these two options, we will present, from here onwards, the decision-making criteria in the context of the utilization of Orchestra Networks' Model-driven MDM EBX Platform[6].

10.5. Derivation procedures

We are now going to describe the derivation procedures used for the semantic classes, then the business operations.

10.5.1. *Derivation of the semantic classes*

The nested data types are systematically removed at the borders of the domains of business objects and data categories. They can be removed even inside the data categories for ergonomic reasons (see Table 10.1). When a nested data type is removed, it is replaced by a key or a list of foreign keys according to the data cardinality designed at the semantic level. The use of multi-valued attributes is possible as the data analyst is not obliged to respect the normal forms of the relational oriented approach.

---

5. That is to say, type of data which declares a primary key (PK).
6. http://www.orchestranetworks.com/

	Complex data type	**Table** (data structure with primary key)

Example	Client #1
	  Number
	  Name
	  First name
	  Command #1
	    Number
	    Xxx
	    Xxx
	  Command #2
	    Number
	    Xxx
	    Xxx
	  Command #3
	    Number
	    Xxx
	    Xxx
		Client #1
		  Number <<Primary Key>>
		  Name
		  First name
		  ListofCommand [*] <<ForeignKey>>
		
		Association (relation)
		
		Command
		  Number <<Primary Key>>
		  Xxx
		  Xxx

	In the example on the left, we could call the Client data type a Table with a Primary Key as the client identifier, which does not change the facts presented below about intertwining Order data type.	
Access to data	Access to the nested data is only possible through the root data type. The nested data are trapped in the root type.	There are no constraints on access to data. The keys (PK, FK) allow direct access to all the data. Once the information is modeled in the form of tables, it can be restored via a smart view, meaning filtering through criteria, restricting the attributes displayed, etc.
Ergonomic display	*Display of hierarchical data structures.* It is not possible to filter data occurrences presented (there is no "where" predicate). The user sees all the information in a single block, at the same time as the main structure (root data type) and the intertwined structures, which can be of interest in certain ergonomic contexts. Consulting this type of information becomes difficult when there are more than three levels of nested data types.	*Display of tables and relations between tables via detailed views.* The tool proposes a default navigation link for each many-to-many associations, and it is possible to provide for the opposite (bidirectional navigation through associations). The declaration, in the XML schema, of a "where" predicate expressed in the form of an Xpath allows for a filter, so that the user can restrict the list of information presented through each association.

	Complex data type	**Table** (data structure with primary key)
In case of multi-occurrence	A multi-occurrence nested data type is limited in terms of the number of occurrences presented on a screen. There are no systems of pagination. The loading of a page can slow down response time.	A Table is a multi-occurrence data type without any limitations on display, since a pagination mechanism is managed by the tool. Display performance remains stable.
Triggering processing	It is possible to attach operations to a complex data type by linking the type to an implementation class (Java).	A table can accept the declaration of triggers, both pre- and post-operation on CRUD services.

Table 10.1. *Comparison between the use of complex data types and tables (PK: Primary Key; FK: Foreign Key)*

Indeed, the target being a Model-driven MDM system, the latter is capable of retaining the multi-valued attributes by ensuring data integrity: it automates the adoption of normal forms of the relational oriented approach. This also has an impact on the derivation of many-to-many associations because it becomes possible to hide join tables. From these starting principles, the derivation rules of semantic classes towards a logical data model cover numerous cases of modeling, notably the following:

– association oriented inside the same category;

– association oriented in different categories;

– association not oriented in the same category;

– association not oriented between different categories;

– qualified association (qualifier attribute);

– recursive association;

– composition in the same category;

– composition between different categories;

– aggregation in the same category;

– aggregation between different categories;

– associative class;

– ternary association in the same category;

– ternary association between different categories;

– inheritance in the same category;

– inheritance between different categories; etc.

10.5.2. *Examples of derivation of semantic classes*

We cannot give all the derivation rules in this book, but we refer the reader to the MDM modeling procedures guide, downloadable on the MDM Alliance Group website, to consult them in full.[7] To illustrate these derivations, we will now give a couple of cases taken from this guide.

10.5.2.1. *Many-to-many association spanning two data categories*

Multiple associations (one-to-many, many-to-many) are not derived with the help of join tables, as is done in the relational oriented approach. From an ergonomic point of view, a specific screen for each join table would be required. These screens are not meaningful for business users and not very ergonomic to browse links between data. It is preferable to directly use a multi-occurrence attribute to declare a list of Foreign Keys as is possible with the object oriented approach, and then to hide underlying join tables. A Model-driven MDM is able to automatically manage these types of multi-occurrence attributes which avoid useless bespoke software development to hide join tables on the user interface of an MDM.

---

7. http://www.mdmalliancegroup.com. The appendix of the guide details these derivation rules.

In the logical data model, many-to-many bi-directional associations must be avoided as they can become complex to interpret at the ergonomic level. We prefer instead to establish an orientation, that which is most natural for the user, even if it is not specified at the semantic modeling level. In Figure 10.3, the association is oriented from Class A to Class B which defines the direction to browse the link.

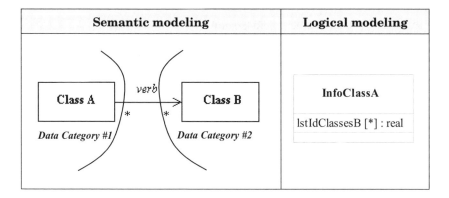

Figure 10.3. *Derivation of a many-to-many association spanning two data categories*

10.5.2.2. *Qualifier attribute*

The qualifier attribute enables class occurrences "ClassB" to be filtered through the association starting from ClassA. This is an enumeration data type. In this case, the logical modeling brings a composite foreign key (in this example: InfoRole2FK).

This derivation rule does not depend on the frontiers of data categories.

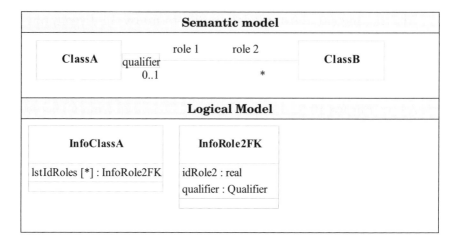

Figure 10.4. *Qualifier attribute derivation*

10.5.2.3. *Recursive association*

In the case of recursive association derivation, the use of nested data types is straightaway put aside due to the recursion. Therefore, Foreign Keys are used.

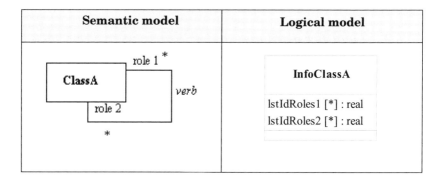

Figure 10.5. *Recursive association derivation*

10.5.2.4. *Associative class in the same category*

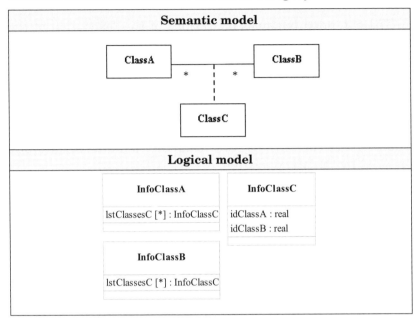

Figure 10.6. *Associative class derivation within the same category*

Each occurrence of the associative class "ClassC" exists for a single couple "ClassA" and "ClassB". The logical data modeling brings to light the use of keys for the data type, "InfoClassC", and multi-occurrence nested data types for "InfoClassA" and "InfoClassB".

10.5.3. *Derivation of elementary business operations*

Elementary business operations overload the CRUD services brought by the MDM system and ensured by default with each business object. The designer assembles the elementary business operations in order to declare them in the form of a single service, located in pre- or post-condition of CRUD services implicated in modifications that must be made.

10.5.4. *Derivation of extended business operations*

The extended business operations of the "execution of the transition" type are retaken by the designer so that the extended use cases can invoke them[8].

The extended business operations of the "pre-condition of modification" type and "control of the change of state value" type are implemented, all the while profiting from a decision table. These operations overload the default functioning ensured by the MDM system.

Multi-occurrence business operations are services which are invoked independently of the unitary CRUD services ensured by default by the MDM system. Their execution requires that the user select, beforehand, a set of occurrences of a business object.

10.5.5. *Derivation of inheritance*

The case of class inheritance, that can exist at the semantic modeling level, are "unfolded" profiting a composition of data types. The MDM system, as for relational oriented systems, can generally not tackle a direct management of data inheritances.

Classically, the three following scenarios are at our disposal to derive an inheritance data structure at the logical level. The designer decides on the best option following the needs and desired optimizations:

– a table per class;

– a table per concrete class;

– a table for all the classes.

---

8. See Chapters 8, 9 and 11 for the definition of extended business operations and extended use cases.

10.5.6. *Identifier management*

A common practice is to put a technical key in place from which referential integrity constraints are exercised. This way, it is possible to modify the business identifier without impacting the referential integrity constraints already in place.

In a context where the business identifiers are stable, it is not necessary to put this mechanism in place; this should be the case when the MDM system is put into practice. The rules of identifier creation are specified, particularly if their computation is generated automatically.

10.5.7. *Calculated information*

The calculated information (derived attribute), identified at a semantic modeling level, is retaken in the form of services that must be executed when accessing the attribute corresponding to this information.

10.6. Other logical modeling procedures

In this section we give an insight into the following procedures: enumeration data type, user message, user interface component, data documentation, and naming rules.

10.6.1. *Enumeration data type*

Each enumeration (code and value) coming from the semantic model is replaced by management in a dedicated table or in a unified table of the MDM which absorbs several data enumerations[9].

---

9. The same approach as from the data enumerations in the provenance of organizational models (Chapter 11).

A unified table can be used to assemble all the data enumerations that have low occurrence numbers, less than a hundred or so values, in order to avoid a proliferation of tables with low volume.

For instance, an information "Market type" is an enumeration data at the semantic modeling level with the values "USA | UK | International". On the other hand, at the logical modeling level, this information is transformed in the form of:

– a dedicated table to benefit an autonomous governance of this information, particularly its versions and rights permissions; or

– an implementation in a unified table which absorbs several data enumerations. This table has complementary information at its disposal that enables the determination of the classification of each code and value; in our example this is the "Market type". This solution avoids multiplying tables with low volume that have a common structure and data governance.

10.6.2. *User message*

The operations can prompt information and error messages.

These messages must be treated as enumerations data managed by the MDM system. Therefore, they benefit from an initialization and update by use context, in particular multi-languages, and benefit from version management.

10.6.3. *User interface components*

For certain ergonomic needs, the man–machine interface offered by default by the Model-driven MDM system must be extended. For example, a credit rate can be the object of an initialization through a rate grid rather than in the form of a classic input field. In this case, it is convenient, at the time of logical modeling, to specify these user interface components in view of preparing their realization in the software.

10.6.4. *Data documentation*

Data documentation, following the ISO/CEI 11179 norm,[10] is managed by a data repository under the control of the MDM system. The model of this repository takes the description of logical data and enriches them with the meta-data defined in ISO/CEI 11179.

10.6.5. *Naming rules*

The data naming used for logical modeling must immediately be reusable in the software, that is to say in the XML (XSD) data schemas. We could opt for a more independent approach to logical data naming, but that would mean managing a translation at the time of production of XML schemas, which would make the chain of production more complex. The isolation of the modeling vis-à-vis technical solutions is already acquired by the upstream semantic (business) and pragmatic (organization) models that enable this technical adherence to be admitted in the logical models. In reality, the adherence is low, since the possibilities in data naming in XML schema are not restrictive. A CAMEL[11] case, with extended labels (without white space or accented characters) is generally adopted.

Putting in place a dictionary of prefixes enabling certain types of reference and master data to be distinguished is recommended: date (dt), label (lb), identifier (id), number (no), etc.

---

10. http://metadata-standards.org/11179/
11. i.e. using upper and lower cases to distinguish terms, e.g. ProductName, DataSource, costOfTheInitialDisaster, etc.

Chapter 11

Organization Modeling

Organization modeling is all about data approval processes and use cases. It is necessary to distinguish:

– their specification, from a requirement point of view, also called "pragmatic modeling"[1];

– the derivation of the pragmatic models in logical terms, which make sense of the MDM software tool.

The pragmatic modeling procedures are simpler than those which have already been proposed for semantic modeling. The modeling effort required by an MDM system is concerned first and foremost with data domains and less with organization domains. Consequently, the study of processes and use cases does not pose a problem in modeling, on condition that the aspects relative to the core business are not integrated within it, as these are dealt with exclusively in the semantic modeling. It is necessary to bear in mind that the more robust and detailed semantic modeling is, the more modeling of processes and use cases is simple.

---

1. In terms of the Praxeme method, organization modeling corresponds to the "pragmatic aspect" of its Enterprise System Topology. See also Chapter 8.

Therefore, it is preferable to begin organization modeling only after the semantic models are available and valid.

These procedures benefit from the Praxeme method, readily made available by the Praxeme Institute.

As for semantic modeling, the pragmatic modeling procedures form a toolkit destined at the same time for business users and the IT department.

11.1. The components of pragmatic modeling

Pragmatic modeling is built around three components:

– the "processes" model, in the form of a succession of steps, the coordination of work between actors involved in the use of the MDM system. This is a data approval process, handled by a workflow, with a task list that notifies the players of the operations that need to be carried out;

– the "use cases" model the interactions of one actor with the MDM system[2], in the form of a succession of activities that participate in the execution of an operation. The use cases can generally be reduced to a single activity that answers a model such as: display of a screen, data input and data validation;

– the "administrative objects" represent the information relative to the organization, like, for example, the permission data of a system, the meta-data used to manage archiving data. They are equivalent to business objects in semantic modeling but their reach is more organizational than core business.

We will now provide the modeling procedures for each of these components.

---

2. An actor is either a human operator, or an IT system.

11.2. Data approval processes

The data approval process is modeled in the same way as any process with a more extended scope than just an MDM system. We will now illustrate the mechanism of this type of process with the help of an example that deals with the modification of a product's tariff.

11.2.1. *Process example*

Figure 11.1 is a simplified example of a data approval process which involves two human actors (sales manager, product manager) and a system actor (data quality for product). It is an Activity Diagram in UML; reading it does not require an in depth knowledge of the UML notation.

Each step of Figure 11.1 corresponds to an MDM use case, except for "checking price quality" which is carried out by a data quality tool, located outside the MDM system. This process is entirely piloted by a workflow, either integrated in the MDM tool, or outside it. The data flow between two steps corresponds to the posting of a task into the task list of the human actor who is the recipient of the flow, or in the queue of the targeted system.

The sales manager is in charge updating the pricing of products. He takes on the role of Data Steward[3]; he is responsible for data updates by product. The tariff modification is possible only if the state of the "product" business object allows it. This constraint is visible in the form of the state "Validated in the reference branch", which means that the product must be in the "validated" business state in the reference branch of the version management. This branch has the current version of the product description[4]. The first action led by the sales manager is the

3. See Chapter 7 for a detailed definition of roles.
4. See Chapter 6 for a reminder of the principles of version management.

creation of a working branch with which it can configure the
new tariff without altering the current product description.
In other words, it creates a copy of the product that is visible
in the diagram through the "validated in the working
branch" outcome. This step uses a governance function of the
MDM system related to version management. All the
remaining steps of the process work on this working version
of the product.

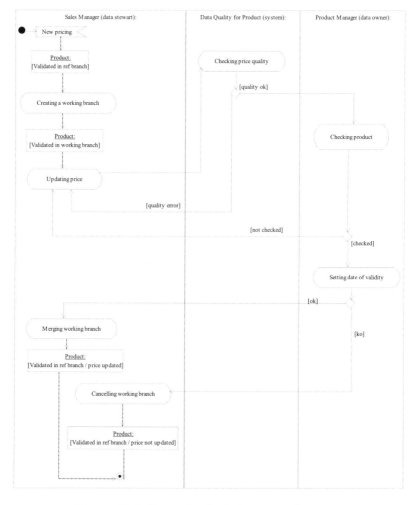

Figure 11.1. *Example of a data approval process*

Following a data update, the workflow launches the execution of a product quality tool, for instance to detect errors in the new pricing or mismatches with other similar product tariffs. The "Data Quality for Product" actor embodies the system discussed by the process; this is a system actor. As soon as the validation of a new pricing is achieved, the process requests a final validation and the input of a validity date for this new tariff by the product manager. This request is dealt with by the workflow that posts the validation demand and the data input in the task list of the product manager. The product manager takes on the role of Data Owner.

As Data Owner, it is common for the product manager to be implicated, as a last resort, for the validation of a new tariff. If this agreement is pronounced, then the workflow continues the execution of the process by asking the sales manager to go ahead with the merging of the working branch, i.e. the product copy, with the reference branch in order to apply the new tariff. In order to do this, the sales manager uses the MDM governance functions enabling the merging of versions. On the process diagram, this step is marked as "merging working branch". At the end of this merging, the product has a new tariff. By contrast, if the product manager cannot decide on the validity date of a new tariff, then it is cancelled. In that case, the workflow asks the sales manager to delete the working branch, which has no effect on the reference branch and therefore on the current description of the product which keeps its current tariff.

This illustration confirms that modeling of the data approval process uses principles already known when the workflow approach is taken: human and system actors, states succession, notification via use of the task lists by actors, predicates on the business objects' states. The MDM approach additionally takes into account data governance functions, like version management, essential in order to coordinate the data modifications.

11.2.2. *Synchronization of use cases with processes*

The use cases are triggered with the help of two devices:

– directly by the screens or the application programming interface of the MDM (pull mode from the user);

– using the workflow as an intermediate, i.e. via a task list inviting the user to execute the use cases on which the system is asking him to act (push mode from the system).

Before the launch of a use case via the MDM system, it is necessary to ensure that a process executed by the workflow is not already running for the handled business object in this use case. Indeed, certain situations can arise where the process which is running blocks the execution of certain use cases. For instance, an ongoing process of tariff negotiation can lead to preventing the setting off, by the MDM system, of the "modify the product" use case.

This synchronization is necessary as it is not possible to force the MDM system users to uniquely work in the processes, i.e. in the setting off of the use cases pushed by the workflow into a task list. Such an approach would mean modeling all the data approval processes, which is usually neither possible nor desirable. It is better to model the key processes and let the users, respecting rights permission, set off the use cases depending on needs.

Consequently, it is necessary to verify, with the launch of each use case, whether or not it is susceptible of being constrained by an ongoing process. To achieve this, the MDM system uses a decision table that enables the synchronization to be automated[5].

This decision table is master data; it is therefore governed by the MDM system and benefits from use contexts management and the version management (see Chapter 6).

11.2.3. *The other processes*

Beyond data approval, other processes need to be taken into consideration, in particular the following:

– initial data loading, often coupled with data cleaning tools before injection into the MDM system;

– management of the lifecycle of the data repository throughout the technical environments: development, unit tests, user acceptance tests, training, pre-production, production, etc.;

– integration of the MDM system with the rest of the information system.

The modeling procedures for these processes are the same as those used for data approval. The modeling is carried out from the pragmatic aspect when they depend on the organization. In the opposite case, they are dealt with at the time of logical modeling.

11.3. Use cases

A use case describes the interaction of one actor with the MDM system over the same timeframe. Unlike processes, there is no task lists management; the workflow does not intervene. We will see that an approach via the

---

5. For example, for each step of a data approval process, the decision table provides the list of the forbidden use cases for a direct setting off by user interface actions or programming services of the MDM system.

documentation of the use cases is sufficient: it is not necessary to carry out a formal modeling such as that practiced for transactional systems. At the same time, we will distinguish the use cases that are carried out by default through the MDM (elementary use case) and those that require a bespoke development (extended use case).

11.3.1. *Documentation of use cases*

For the MDM system, modeling of a use case is exceptional as they follow, most of the time, a simple interaction model such as: screen display, data input, and data validation. In other words, we are dealing with CRUD type interactions to manage the Creation, the Reading, the Update and the Deletion of business objects. With the exception of read use cases, the others generally work on the scope of a single business object, with a transaction management which is limited to it.

For example, the MDM system has "modify product" and "modify factory" use cases that are each executed following a simple interaction, that of display, data input and data validation. It is rare to dispose of a use case capable of proceeding at the same time to the modification of products and factories in a same transaction. In this case, the system is further away from its reference and master data vocation to achieve a transactional application. It would then be necessary to specify the synchronization rules between the product modifications and factory modifications, as well as screens and interaction steps enabling the user to successfully achieve the transaction.

Consequently, rather than modeling, it is more convenient to document the use cases in the following manner:

– name, in a verbal form;

– type: create, read, update, delete;

– business object handled in the case of create, update and delete. A business objects list is possible in the read case;

– permissions management: i.e. the organizational conditions that enable its execution. This is the access rights but also the enforcement rules of these rights such as, especially, the thresholds applied to certain data. For example, an actor is empowered to delete products (access rights) except those which have a price superior to a certain threshold (enforcement rules);

– context management: i.e. the variants to apply to this use case. This translates to a hiding of certain data that we do not wish to use in the execution of the use case, depending on the context. For example, we can have a use case "Party entry" and filter the company name and the company registration number for the context of an individual party. Another type of filter can be necessary when a use case is set off by the workflow: the process limits the action required by the user; rather than present the totality of the business object data, the context enables a screen dedicated to the work that the user must carry out to be built. For example, if the process is asking for the modification of the contact details of a client, it is not necessary that the MDM system screen present all the data of this client; it is better to create a variant on the "modify client" use case limited to the management of the contact details.

This documentation must not be formulated in an informal manner, with the help of a word processor. It would be too verbose, difficult to maintain and not synchronized with the software. On the other hand, all the characteristics of these use cases are master data that can be entered into the MDM system. It is then necessary to establish a use cases repository. If the MDM system tool is properly studied then it already integrates this repository or enables it to be built in an accelerated manner: introspection of business object data and filtering by use contexts (through decision tables), permission management, naming of use cases (verbal base), etc.

This configuration data is automatically taken into consideration by the MDM system to generate screens and adapt the behavior of its programming services.

The approach described here functions if the use cases of the MDM system respect a generic interaction model. We call this an "elementary use case".

We leave room for rare use cases that go beyond the generic model and name them "extended use cases". The following sections return to the definition and realization of these two types of use cases.

11.3.2. *Elementary use case*

A use case is elementary when it is executed in the ergonomic mechanism provided by default by the MDM system for the creation, reading, modification and deletion.

To achieve this, this use case can call upon elementary business operations, i.e. those that don't have dependencies on the business objects' states. It can also execute extended business operations, but only those that do not modify the business objects' states. The execution of these operations is then constrained by the states decision table (see previous chapter on semantic modeling).

Consequently, the elementary use case can never call upon a business operation that is susceptible to change the state of a business object. The impact of a state modification is of such importance for data integrity that it is important not to, from an organizational point of view, enable its execution in such as generic manner as the elementary use case. It is a reason why we need the extended use case concept.

11.3.3. *Extended use case*

A use case is extended when it enables the user to change a business object's state. This use case requires an extended business operation which is a transition applied to the business object's state machine. A transition is a progression from one state to another.

The importance of the user action is such that the unique CRUD actions, on offer by default in the MDM system, are no longer sufficient.

The extended use case is presented to the user in the form of a named action (verbal group of the use case) specifying the impact on the state of the business object which is being handled.

For example, if it is about evolving an "engine" business object in an "in repair" state, we then have a "go for repair" use case. If a specific man–machine dialog is necessary, such as the display of a confirmation demand or the input of additional data, for example the number of the workshops in charge of repairs, then the use case gives the specification for this[6].

11.4. Administrative objects

Administrative objects bring together information that is not dependent on the core business. They concern, for example, permission data of systems, organizational structures, meta-data used to manage data archiving, data for managing the data flows mapping between systems, etc.

---

6. This specification can be carried out with the help of a state machine, defining the steps of the dialog, linked to the use case; for more information on this modeling procedure see the pragmatic aspect of the Praxeme method (www.praxeme.org).

These objects are modeled with the help of the same procedures as those already described for business objects, in semantic modeling. In particular, a first-level data architecture can be identified around administrative object domains. Just as for business object domains, they form the first access levels in the MDM tool, at the time of data governance.

In certain cases, the MDM tool proposes administrative objects ready for use, for permission data applied to reference and master data, data approval workflow, the management of use contexts applied to use cases, etc. This further relieves the modeling of administrative objects.

11.5. The derivation of pragmatic models to logical models

The derivation of the pragmatic aspect to the logical aspect does not require a logical modeling of use cases. They are described as formal documentation associated with decision tables (see above). The data approval processes are translated in terms comprehensible to the workflow engine used. Only the administrative objects require a logical modeling of data, the same as that already described for business objects that come from the semantic models.

11.5.1. *Use cases*

We have already seen that the use case, in the MDM approach, does not require UML modeling. Its behavior is described in the form of data configuration directly governed in the MDM system and exploited by it for the automatic adaptation of its screens and taking permission management into consideration.

Consequently, there is no logical modeling to foresee for use cases.

11.5.2. *Data approval process*

Logical modeling takes the pragmatic approval processes in order to make clear their specifications by taking into account the retained workflow tool. It can be a workflow available in the MDM system or a generic exterior workflow. This modeling is reduced and is limited to configuration rules in the workflow.

11.5.3. *Administrative object*

The logical modeling of data follows the same rules as those retained by semantic modeling (see Chapter 10).

11.5.4. *Transaction*

For operations that require a bespoke transactional scope, it is necessary to foresee the following mechanisms:

– piloting of transactional opening and closure (begin, commit) by a simple operation configuration. When an operation fails, then the rollback is automatically pronounced. In other words, each operation has meta-data that enables it to decide, depending on the requirements of its transactional behavior. Therefore, the same operation can be transactional in an MDM execution context, and not in another context;

– management of nested transactions. In order to manage transactions on a scope going beyond a simple CRUD applied to a single business object, it is necessary to configure the master/slave functioning of nested transactional operations. For example, the update operation of a product is master vis-a-vis other guarantee update operations which are then slaves. In other words, the beginning and the end of the transaction is carried by the first operation; the others called upon during its execution do not open up the transaction.

Finally, the data updates must be executed in the context of a single man–machine interaction as it is always preferable to forbid floating transactions on several interaction screens. Therefore, we avoid a transaction starting on one screen and not ending, as the commit phase is found on a further screen which the user has not activated.

Chapter 12

Technical Integration of an MDM system

We are now going to bring together several important aspects of the technical integration of an MDM system with the rest of an information system. First of all, we will describe three integration models, with successively weak coupling, tight coupling and loose coupling.

We will also show how to correct the usual weaknesses in pivot formats used at the EAI/ESB level of benefiting from the semantic modeling already carried out for the MDM system. We will describe in detail how the repository is put to work for a better governance of exchanges between systems, followed by synchronization mechanisms with other databases and, finally, its integration with the Business Rules Management System (BRMS). We will end this chapter with a proposal for the classification of databases (relational OLTP *versus* semantic) coupled with the development techniques (traditional *versus* Model-driven) in order to take into consideration the differences between the integration of an OLTP MDM and a Model-driven MDM system.

12.1. Integration models

The integration of the MDM system with the rest of the system is described at the time of logical modeling. Business and organization models must not be impacted by this work. However, it is necessary to avoid a situation in which models could not be properly translated at the time of logical modeling, because of technical constraints.

In particular, the following points need to be considered:

– impact of the functional and technical silo architecture on the modeling of data approval processes. Certain steps in these processes can appear under the constraints of silo boundaries and data synchronization options. For example, a financial classification is created in a silo and then sent, in a batch mode, to the MDM system to be referenced and validated. If the MDM system rejects this classification, it is then necessary to foresee an organizational step, enabling an actor to deal with the problem. This step is no longer useful if the synchronization with the MDM system is carried out in real time since the validation is done at the time of input;

– reinforcement of the business object states is used to synchronize the MDM system with the other databases. For example, a "product" business object, governed in the repository, is synchronized with the manufacturing system as soon as its business state changes from "to be configured" to "configured".

Consequently, as soon as the MDM approach is started, it is necessary to decide upon the integration model which is to be used for the future data repository (see Figure 12.1).

The objective is not to burden the business and organization modeling with technical preoccupations but to prepare the way in which their logical derivation will be carried out. Figure 12.1 shows this decision stage and also recalls that it is necessary to decide, before starting logical modeling, the style of the MDM system retained: either a classic MDM system based on a relational OLTP database, or an MDM system that benefits from a rich data model enabling a Model-driven MDM system to be started[1].

We will see, in the rest of this chapter, that the Model-driven approach also conditions the integration of the MDM system with the rest of the information system.

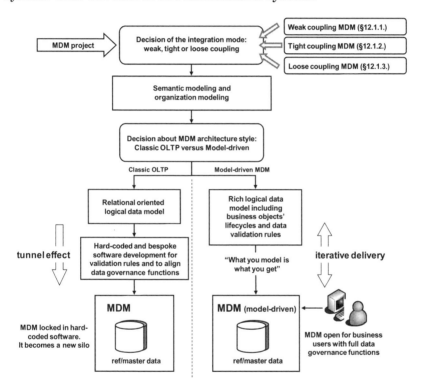

Figure 12.1. *Integration models decided at the start of the MDM approach and the choice of MDM architecture style*

---

1. A Model-driven MDM completes the usual functioning of relational dabase systems; see Chapter 5.

The decision surrounding the integration models is based around three possible approaches: weak coupling, tight coupling and loose coupling. We now describe each of them.

12.1.1. *Weak coupling*

In this integration model, the MDM system is used in a desynchronized manner. The following example shows the behavior of weak coupling during the update of a Customer's within a CRM (Customer Relationship Management) system.

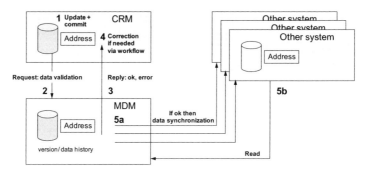

Figure 12.2. *Weak MDM coupling*

The customer relationship management system ensures the address management (stage 1), in an autonomous fashion and within its own transactional scope. At the same time, it sends the new address or the modification of an already existing address to the MDM system, so that the repository validates it and ensures version and history management (stage 2). If the address is valid, then the MDM system immediately diffuses it towards other systems that are supposed to use the address at its most accurate value (stage 5a) and meets the consultation needs (stage 5b). On the other hand, if the MDM system does not validate the address then it sends an error message to the CRM system that must be able to correct it (stages 3 and 4) and the other systems are not updated.

For this integration model to work, it is imperative that the lifecycle of the "address" business object is modeled. The state of the address has different values depending on its synchronization level between the MDM and other systems: to be validated, validated, to be completed, etc.

This is a weak coupling model as the MDM availability does not condition the execution of other systems, at least as long as the updates must not be propagated immediately.

12.1.2. *Tight coupling*

In this integration model, the MDM system is synchronized in real time with the other systems.

Applied to the management of the address, Figure 12.3 shows the synchronization that should be implemented.

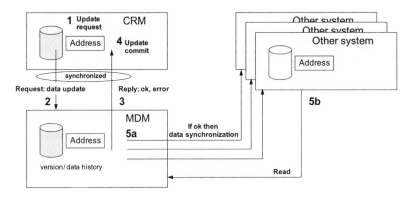

Figure 12.3. *Tight coupling MDM*

In this scenario, the CRM is not autonomous. It cannot manage the addresses without being synchronized beforehand with the MDM system; the MDM system is then a single point of failure. In other words, if the MDM system is not available, the CRM can no longer manage addresses.

This MDM system is in tight coupling because its availability is crucial for the execution of other systems that update and use master data.

12.1.3. *Loose coupling*

In this last integration model, the MDM system is not directly used in the production environment. The repository is duplicated in the databases that use the reference and master data in production.

For example, product configuration is carried out in an environment dedicated to configuration. Once the configuration has been validated, the products are replicated in the databases of the transactional in-house systems and software packages. These systems do not have a direct relation with the MDM system.

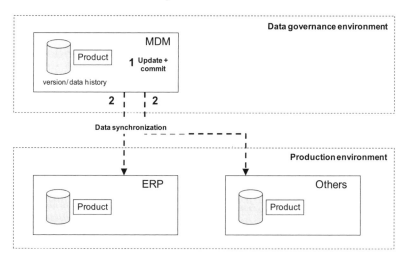

Figure 12.4. *Loose coupling*

This MDM is in loose coupling vis-à-vis other systems as it is not localized in a production environment.

12.1.4. *Consequences of integration models*

The three models that we have just described can co-exist within the same information system, at the same time for different MDM repositories, but also for the same MDM repository.

For example, an address repository can base itself on a tight coupling MDM system as long as its availability permits it, and then automatically swing to a loose coupling MDM system in case of unavailability, in order not to block the transactional systems.

Table 12.1 draws up a comparison between the three integration models.

Characteristics	Weak Coupling	Tight Coupling	Loose Coupling
The synchronization between the MDM system and other databases is done by benefiting from the management of the lifecycle of data	Obligatory	Strongly recommended	Strongly recommended
The availability of the MDM system conditions the execution of other systems	No	Yes	No
The propagation of the MDM update towards other databases is done in real time	No	Yes	No
The MDM system is used in the production environment	Yes	Yes	No
Real-time read access to the MDM system is possible	Yes	Yes	No
Real-time update access to the MDM system is possible	No	Yes	Yes
The MDM system performance problems impact those of other systems	No	Yes	No

Table 12.1. *A summary of the MDM integration models*

The constraints induced by these integration models on the business modeling (semantic) and on the organization modeling (pragmatic) are expressed primarily on two levels:

– first of all, by the reminder of the importance of the modeling of the business objects' lifecycles (first line of Table 12.1). In particular, a MDM system in weak coupling means the management of states in order to synchronize, in a reliable manner, the data with the rest of the information system. In other words, the integration model in weak coupling reaffirms the necessity of opting for the "semantic MDM" maturity level, uniquely capable of taking into consideration the management of states as master data (see Chapter 5);

– then, the data approval processes may have to take into account organizational steps imposed by the technical integration of the repository. For example, with the weak coupling MDM system, if the address is not validated by the MDM system, it is necessary to push a request in the task list of a CRM actor in order to correct the problem. This organizational step exists only if the integration model used is that of an MDM in weak coupling.

12.2. Semantic integration

The three integration models that we have just described require the use of a software layer in charge of data exchanges between systems; generally, this is a communication bus or Enterprise Service Bus (ESB) .To avoid this bus becoming a connection nightmare, a "point to point" between systems, it is necessary to implement a pivot format of data. Unfortunately, most of the time, this format is specified in an incremental manner, as new data exchange needs appear. As time goes by, the pivot format piles up data structure duplications and has no well-documented data validation rules. Just like functional and technical silos, we find in the integration layer a stratification that generates unnecessary complexity, i.e. without direct relation to the data exchange needs.

This weakness is inevitable if the teams in charge of the ESB do not have the means or the competency to lead data modeling, across the whole of the information system, to fruition. This is almost always the case; the ESB is perceived as a technical solution that leaves no room to budget for data modeling. With the MDM approach, the situation changes radically. Indeed, semantic modeling becomes unavoidable. The effort dedicated to data modeling, across the whole information system, is justified by the MDM approach. Even though it is only concerned with reference and master data, it requires, beforehand, the implementation of a common enterprise data architecture that embraces reference/master data and transactional data at the same time (see Chapter 8).

From then on, since a rich data model is available, it becomes evident that it is necessary to reuse it instead of usual pivot formats which have inferior data quality. This has the following advantages:

– since the data model is based on a common enterprise data architecture foundation, its stability over time is reinforced. The business objects domains, data categories and business objects are stable and shared across the all the information systems (see Chapter 8). The degradation of the pivot formats, caused by a progressive stratification of data structures, no longer exists;

– we have seen that the maturity level of a "semantic MDM" system takes into consideration the dynamic modeling of data, in particular the lifecycles of business objects and data validation rules. The classic hard-coded software development of the data validation rules outside the pivot formats is reduced. Consequently, the rich data model raises the auditability of data; business users have greater ease in querying and governing data flows between systems.

Beyond reference and master data, the exchanges between systems concern transactional data. The latter must also benefit from a more rich and stable data model than the unique pivotal format. The modeling of this data is carried out, progressively, by also basing itself on a common foundation brought about by business object domains, data categories and business objects.

From a physical point of view, the data model is derived in the form of an XML schema[2] used in the following manner:

– in its entirety, in the integration layer in order to obtain a "semantic mapping". The canonical representation ensured by this schema rationalizes and renders more reliable the data transformations between systems;

– the subset that is relevant to reference and master data is injected in the MDM system.

This reinforcement of modeling in the integration level dramatically changes the way in which the data transformations are carried out. It results in the concept of "semantic integration".

---

2. The XML Schema standard accepts extensions, which enables it to take into consideration all the necessary directives to implement, at a physical level, rich data models, without losing information. See for example, the extensions proposed by the Model-driven MDM EBX Platform from Orchestra Networks. An extension case concerns the dynamic management of data cardinality minOccurs and maxOccurs, managed like master data rather than frozen values in the schema. Another case concerns taking primary and foreign keys into consideration, essential to express the associations between business objects and their referential integrity constraints.

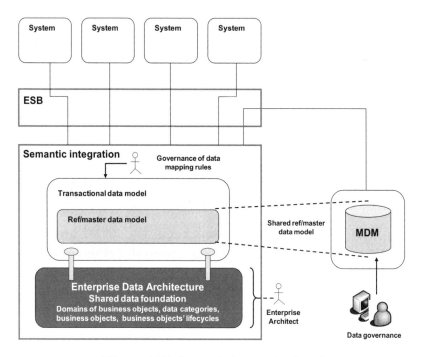

Figure 12.5. *Semantic integration benefits*
from the MDM approach

Semantic integration is a considerable lever effect to transform semantic modeling as a return on investment. On the condition of using a "semantic integration" software solution[3] capable of working with a rich data model, the rationalization of data exchanges and the optimization of ESB management are improved. At the same time that the MDM approach, the company benefits, with no added modeling cost, from an improved management of exchanges between systems (Figure 12.5).

---

3. See Progress Software "DataXtend" at
http://web.progress.com/dataxtend/index.html

12.3. Data synchronization

The quality of the synchronization procedures between an MDM system and other databases conditions the success of the MDM approach. This approach must not be mistaken for integration models that we saw earlier. Indeed, once the coupling level (weak, tight, loose) has been chosen, it is also necessary to determine the synchronization level: does each data modification in the MDM system mean a synchronization with the rest of the IS or is it necessary to group several modifications together?

In most cases, companies that begin the MDM approach wrongly perceive only two levels of synchronization, with:

– batch treatments which bring together significant volumes of data, with a daily or superior periodicity; or

– each elementary data modification.

This perception is not sufficient enough as the synchronization of data executed to each elementary modification leads, generally, to a technical dead end in the ESB. Too many update events circulate on the communication bus. The teams in charge of the integration then attempt to bring together several events, in order to factorize certain modifications, but without any data modeling to support this effort.

The ESB in this case is used as a buffer in order to avoid the systems being too in demand from the elementary data modifications. These constraints lead IT Architects to favor the batch function mode and limit real time updates, which penalizes the effectiveness of the MDM system. It is possible to correct this situation by profiting from the lifecycles of business objects.

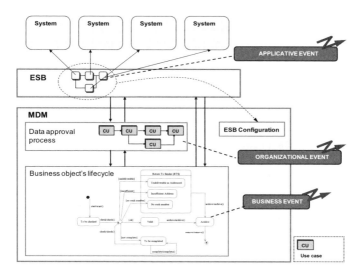

Figure 12.6. *The synchronization of the MDM with the rest of the system*

Indeed, a third level of synchronization exists that intervenes when the states of business objects evolve. For example, during the updates of the characteristics of the "Product" business object in the MDM system, we might want to synchronize the data with other systems only when the product state changes from "to be negotiated" to the "negotiated" state. This new synchronization possibility dramatically changes the way in which the MDM system is synchronized.

Instead of a static repository that must notify the ESB of each of the data modifications, we have a more dynamic MDM system that benefits from the lifecycles of business objects to optimize its relationship with the ESB. Of course, in order to achieve this, it is necessary to implement the maturity level of the "semantic MDM" with a complete modeling of data that is not limited to a static description[4].

---

4. See the state machine example of the business object "Address" described in Chapter 9.

Therefore, it is necessary to take into consideration three types of events to manage, in a reliable manner, the synchronization of the MDM with the rest of the information system (Figure 12.6): business, organizational and applicative events.

12.3.1. *Business event*

This is the changing of states that regulates the lifecycles of business objects. All the data synchronizations cannot be based on a change of states of business objects, but when this possibility exists it is necessary to profit from it to optimize exchanges between the MDM system and other databases. Without a modeling and formal management of states in the MDM, such as we have described in the level of maturity of the "semantic MDM", this optimization is no longer possible, or requires software developments that are hard coded in the MDM system or even directly in the ESB.

12.3.2. *Organizational event*

Organizational events are changes in states conducting the data approval processes. When a validation of a use case is carried out by a system or human actor, the workflow can be informed of it and takes it into account to notify the information to other systems.

12.3.3. *Applicative event*

This type of event is not directly known by the MDM system. The ESB manages tables of correspondence between update demands emitted by the MDM system and events to be published in other systems.

These tables are master data which is also managed in the MDM system; it is the ESB configuration data that also integrates   the   technical   parameters   on   queues, communications protocols, etc.

12.4. Integration with the BRMS

When the validation and calculation rules are too complex to be expressed solely via the syntax of data models (facets, decision tables), it is necessary to anticipate the use of a rules engine in order to counter the hard-coded development.

The rich data model design for the MDM system is reused by the BRMS (Business Rules Management System), on condition that the two software tools operate with the same standard of physical data; the one that needs to be used is XML schema.

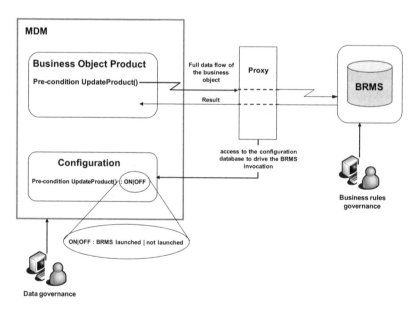

Figure 12.7. *Integration of the MDM system with the BRMS*

In order to ensure a loose coupling between the MDM system and the BRMS, invoking the first towards the second anticipates the sending of a master data flow that collects all the data by business object. The objective is to allow the addition of new rules without modifying the data flow from the MDM system.

For example, in pre-condition of the "person" business object update, all a person's reference and master data are collected in the form of a data flow and then sent to the BRMS. Even if the latter contains only a single validation rule exploiting a few of the person's data, all the flow is sent. In other words, the MDM system does not know rules susceptible to be set off in the BRMS, nor data susceptible to being handled by these rules.

The invocation of the BRMS can also be rendered systematic, for example for all the pre-conditions of the CRUD operations of the MDM system. For a version of the repository, the invoking of the rules engine for a particular operation might not be necessary, even though it could be later. Rather than implement bespoke and hard-coded software to invoke the BRMS, we can anticipate a systematic invocation, even if there are no rules to execute. To avoid unnecessary invocations towards the BRMS, all it takes is to establish a configuration proxy enabling, for each pre-condition of each CRUD operation, whether or not to invoke the rules engine. This configuration table is master data, therefore managed by the MDM system and benefiting from version management and data initialization and update by uses contexts. Consequently, it is possible to configure different behaviors of the repository depending on the contexts, such as subsidiaries, partners, countries, etc., but also by version, such as environments for development, testing, training, production, etc.

The result returned after the execution of rules corresponds to either:

– an assertion. In this case, the pre-condition raises an exception (error) if the assertion is incorrect or continues the execution in the opposite case; or

– a calculation result. In this case, the pre-condition must be able to use this.

The power of the linking of the MDM system with the BRMS is significant. We have presented it here in the sense of data using validation rules. We were able, in the first part of this book, to stress the importance of the association in the opposite sense, i.e. of the BRMS towards the MDM system.

In other words, rules use reference and master data; the reliability and quality of which are at hand in the MDM system; this enables an intensive use of rules with no added technical software development cost usually necessary to retrieve the reference and master data scattered and duplicated across the silos.

12.5. Classification of databases and software development types

The MDM integration process depends greatly on the technology employed. The more the integration is driven by models, the less the hard-coded and bespoke software developments are required. To fully understand the approach by the models applied to the MDM system, it is interesting to know the classification of the databases and development techniques. Figure 12.8 shows the way in which we deal with this classification:

– the horizontal axis gives the intensity of the Model-driven approach; nonexistent with the classic development lifecycle (left); complete with the MDA and Model-driven MDM (right);

– the vertical axis gives the architecture style of the database: classic relational OLTP (bottom); and rich-orientated model (top), i.e. capable of managing behavioral facets, data validation rules, and the lifecycles of business objects (decision table).

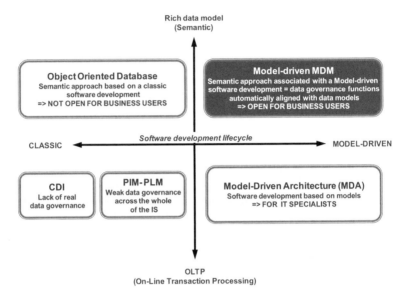

Figure 12.8. *The classification of databases and development techniques*

From these two axes appear four classification zones:

– On-Line Transaction Processing (OLTP) and classic development lifecycle (bottom left quadrant). We find here databases and application software systems developed over the last thirty years. MDM solutions, in this sector, behave like transactional application software, evolving little and not particularly open to data governance by business users. The data model is not very expressive, which means bespoke and hard-coded developments software for the management of the lifecycles of business objects and data validation rules. Repositories such as Customer Data Integration (CDI), Product Information Management (PIM) and Product Lifecycle Management (PLM) are situated in this quadrant;

– OLTP and model driven development lifecycle (bottom right quadrant). This is engineering software driven by models, marked by the Mode-Driven Architecture (MDA) standard of the OMG. This sector does not involve business users; it only concerns IT experts. Consequently, it has no value for MDM;

– semantic and classic development lifecycle (top left quadrant). This is the object oriented database sector. This benefits from a rich data modeling, with the attachment of validation rules. However, the development lifecycle places the solution in the sole hands of IT experts. Consequently, the benefit for MDM is not obvious. Furthermore, performance problems of object oriented databases do not favor their use in transactional solutions. In the end, they are not appropriated for data governance by business users, or for the implementation of transactional solutions. We can understand why the object oriented database does not have significant success in companies;

– semantic and development lifecycle driven by models (top right quadrant). It is in this sector that the association of the rich data models with the model-driven approach gives birth to a new way to implement software solutions. The power of the integration process, from the rich data models, considerably limits hard-coded and bespoke developments software. The involvement of business users is then greater and the data governance functions are automatically aligned with the requirements defined through the models. Applied to the MDM field, it is easy to understand the added-value of this association which results in Model-driven MDM. Just as the performance requirements for the reference and master data governance are less strong than the transactional data, there is no barrier to the use of this technology for an MDM system.

This classification summarizes our book; the association of the MDM system with semantic modeling and the model-driven approach enables the data repository to be fully delivered in agreement with requirements and open for business users. The maturity level of technologies and the method used enable this type of MDM to be practiced, today, on a large scale: this is the Model-driven MDM system.

By practicing Model-driven MDM, a company takes an important first step towards the in-depth transformation of its information system. The investment in data repositories oriented towards businesses users is a strategic choice.

Conclusion

In an increasingly virtual world where execution speed and adaptation is crucial for survival, it is undeniable that IT counts for a lot.

If your company is faced with problems relating to the quality of financial statements, if operational discrepancies appear in your relations with third parties, if you do not know how many times the same client is referenced in your systems, if pricing errors for your services slip into your distribution channels ... then your IT matters.

The refereeing of investments counts even more: why should it be necessary to invest "again" in IT cost centers when the company is better off reinforcing its assets, the valuation of which is immediate (such as the sales force, marketing action to support the brand, or renovation of manufacturing tools, etc.)?

This book briefly touches on this refereeing dilemma concerning IT investments and it is useful to study how budgets are too often used in an incoherent manner.

It is enough to recall recent errors over the past ten years in the Business Process Management (BPM) domain and in data quality:

– unnecessary spending in BPM projects when the processes implemented handle poor quality data;

– unnecessary spending in data quality tools when systems continue to produce poor quality data. These tools act in a loop: they "clean up" databases that silos continue to supply, day to day, with duplicated and erroneous information.

Rather than correct the causes of the weakness of the current Information Systems, too often IT acts on the symptoms. The suppression of a symptom can provide relief in the short term and make it possible to enjoy a rapid gain but the cause remains encrusted in the memory of systems, and is revealed elsewhere, by other actors within the IT system, or later in a more violent manner. The stratification of current systems proves this; the approach of rapid gain is not sustainable.

It is not necessary to engage additional IT budgets to start the renovation. The most important issue is reorientating a part of investments towards dealing more with the causes of weaknesses and less with the symptoms. Of course, this demands a different mobilization of business and IT teams: it is necessary to pool investments, to restart the modeling of needs, not to be content with drawing a process and a few screens to describe a business domain, to acquire competencies or reactivate them, in particular in Master Data Management and in Business Rules Management domains.

The natural temptation of the IT expert is to shy away from tasks involving effort:

– the experienced IT expert seeks the comfort of responsibility for the control of management in maintenance operations, limiting innovation and renovation risks;

– the novice and younger computer scientist is a technological zapper who perceives IT as a technique, of which the modeling appears theoretical, and even (and this is worse) purely academic.

From a business user's perspective, the relation with IT no longer favors the idea of transforming systems. The business actor no longer knows his trade ... he knows the IT tool that is in his hands.

Is it necessary to change your IT system? If it is, then usual practices must seriously be shaken up. This book attempts to contribute to this shake-up by showing a progressive approach that is based on data repositories, the natural pillars of any IT system.

Once the approach is understood, one must admit that we are still missing two tools that have not been described here. It is necessary to have an Information System rating tool[1] that allows decision makers, but also all of the company's stakeholders, from shareholders to employees, to judge the performance of the IS, just as we judge the financial and social performance of a company by the reading of annual reports. It is also necessary to have new fiscal incentives to encourage the reorientation of part of IT investments from maintenance to renovation work.

Putting a MDM system or a BRMS in place, across the whole of the Information System, is a big decision intended to modernize the company's IT, enabling a decrease in the opacity of what is already in place in order to better control the risks and respect regulations. It is necessary to financially encourage companies that choose this path. The idea of a research tax credit on in-depth renovation

---

1. See www.sustainableitarchitecture.com to get a full version of the IS rating tool allowing assessment of IS Assets based on MDM, BRMS and BPM.

investments of IT systems, an essential competitive factor for companies, should become reality. No doubt we will have the opportunity to come back to this in another book dedicated to these aspects.

For the time being, the progression of MDM approaches is already the sign of a beginning of a large transformation in the right direction for IT systems. Companies will invest more and more in data repositories, i.e. in the foundations of their systems.

To take this work further, this book has been accompanied by the creation of the MDM Alliance Group community which makes best practices for a Model-driven MDM and reusable pre-built data models for reference and master data readily available. To keep up-to-date and in contact with the author, and to join the group, visit: http://www.mdmalliancegroup.com.

Appendix

Semantic Modeling of *Address*

This Appendix takes another look at address semantic modeling proposed by the MDM Alliance Group[1]. The objective is to represent the address in a universal manner, with the help of the UML standard. To do this, we define two central semantic concepts:

– the Territory Office, which identifies the administrative territories that distribute mail;

– the Territory, which describes the geography of a country, independently of organizations that distribute the mail.

By associating these two concepts, it is then possible to build addresses depending on the standards of each country (see examples in Table A.1).

It is important to bear in mind that a semantic model is not yet the representation of the database at a logical level, and even less at a physical level.

---

1. www.mdmalliancegroup.com

Example of address	Territory Office	Territory
US 90001	01	900
UK M1 1AA - Several "Territory Offices" are used.	M (postal code), 1 (postal district), 1 (sector), AA (unity)	na
France 69130	130	69

Table A.1. *Address standards for sample countries*

Once the semantic model has been validated, a derivation towards the logical model occurs in order to take into particular account the loose coupling of data (with the help of data categories), their formal naming and performances.

A.1. The semantic model

– The *Period* class specifies the periods of address validity.

– The *Object* class is an abstraction of real world objects: person, building, organization, material assets, etc. All these objects are susceptible to have addresses.

– The *Site* concept enables the declaration of several expressions in a same address depending on the language. This need appears for certain multi-language countries, for instance Belgium. The qualifying attribute *language*, attached to the *Site* class, enables the expression of this mechanism. This possibility could also be useful for the alternative representations of the address, for example in an electronic language.

It is necessary to note that *Site* is an associative class between an object and a period. Consequently, each site instance only exists for one and only one value concept [*Object, Period*].

In a language independent manner, each *Site* can also have geo-localization coordinates at its disposal, following a specific coordinates system (GPS, Galileo, others).

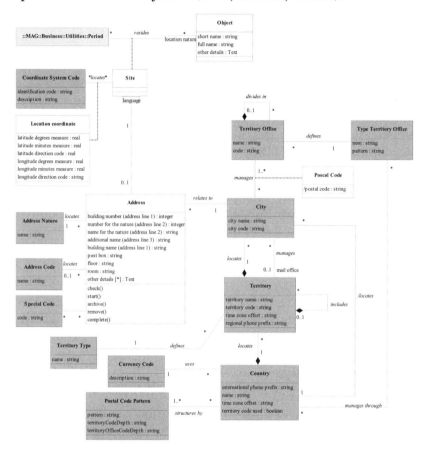

Figure A.1. *Semantic model of the Address object*

– The qualifier attribute *location nature* attached to the *resides* association of the *Object* class specifies the use of the address: professional, personal, secondary, headquarters, delivery, billing, return (place where the client should send back the products in case of a problem), vacation, etc.

– The attributes of the *Address* class do not have functional data dependency. Each address is linked to a *City*, the attachment of which to the *Territory Office* and *Territory* permits the automatic calculation of its postal code, *via* the derived attribute "*/postal code*" of the *Postal Code* class.

– The *Territory Office* is, for example, the postal office for France or the postal zone for the United States.

– In France, the *Territory Office* code consists of three numbers. For example, the town of Orléans has two postal offices: the first for the North of the town (000), and the second for the South (100).

– By prefixing these codes with the *Territory* code (in French: département) it is possible to obtain the postal codes (45 000 and 45 100). For the big cities, these correspond to districts (in French: arrondissements).

In the United States, the *Territory Office* consists of two numbers.

In other countries, the *Territory Office* can be organized differently. For instance, in England, it consists of the concatenation of the postal zone, the district zone, the sector and finally the unit. The reflective association "*divides in*" on the *Territory Office* class enables an expression of this decomposition.

– The values of the *Type of Territory Office* class enumeration depend on the country, for example: postal code for France, postal zone for the US, postal zone, district zone, sector *and* unit for England, etc. The *pattern* attribute enables the declaration of the input format that should be respected, depending on the *Type of Territory Office*.

– The values of the *Territory Type* class enumeration depend on the administrative organization of the territories; for example for France: county (in French: department), region, etc. For the United States: state, county, etc.

– A *Postal Code* class exists for a *City* and *Territory Office* couple; it is an associative class in UML. The "*/postal code*" attribute is automatically calculated for the model, by retrieving the codes of the *Territory Office* and *Territory*, depending on the directives declared in the *Postal Code Pattern* attached to the *Country* corresponding to the *City*.

In certain countries, for example England, the *postal code* is obtained by the unique use of the *Territory Office (Postal Zone + Postal District + Sector + Unity)*. In order to determine whether or not the code of the *Territory* is used, the *territory code depth* attribute of the *Country* class is consequently informed: equal to zero if not used.

– The *Manages* association between *City* and *Territory* classes is declared when the calculation of the *postal code* must take into consideration a special code for the *Territory*.

For example, in France, the town of Laveyrune is situated in the Ardèche (07) region even though its postal code consists of the territory code of Lozère (48). Consequently, the *postal code* of Laveyrune is 48250 even though the territory it is attached to is 07.

– Examples of values for the *Address Nature* list include: *Street, Road, Lane, Boulevard, Way, Building plot*, etc. The values are dependent on the language and the address, in this case English. The data input depending on the use contexts ensured by the Model-driven MDM system enables management of multi-language lists without needing to allow for this device in the semantic model.

– Examples of values for the *Address Code* list include Bis, Quinte, Quater, Ter, etc.

– The *Postal Code Pattern* enables the description of the postal code syntax depending on the country. For example the *length of* the *Territory* code is: France (3 positions), United States (2 positions), Belgium (2 positions). And the total length of the postal code is: France (5 positions), United States (5 positions), Belgium (4 positions). In other words *Postal Code Pattern* class provides the regular expression of the postal code, for each country.

In England, the *Postal Code Pattern* can have several structures. This variability is dealt with by the association *many-to-many* between *Country* and *Postal Code Pattern*.

– The *territory code depth* attribute provides the usage depth of the *Territory*. If the value is zero, this means that the postal code does not take into account the *Territory*; this is the case, for instance, for England.

– The *territory office code depth* attribute provides the usage depth of the *Territory Office*. For England, the value is four, representing the overlap of *Unity*, *Sector*, *Postal district* and *Postal code*. For France, this attribute is equal to one, due to the fact one level of *Territory Office* is sufficient.

– The Special Code class corresponds, for example, to the CEDEX code in France. This code is not obligatory and is added to the end of the address. For the United States, this corresponds to the four letters that complete the ZIP basic code, found under the term *ZIP+4*.

A.2. Examples of screens generated by Model-driven MDM

From this semantic model of the address, a derivation of a logical data model is started in order to take into account the technical implementation and performance aspects. A direct projection of the semantic model in the Model-driven MDM system is also possible, especially to accelerate the modeling validation phases.

The following screens are illustrations of a Model-driven MDM system use with the semantic model of the address[2]. The UML model is translated in the form of an XML schema (XSD) which is imported into the MDM system in order to obtain the data governance screens.

A.2.1. *Postal Code Patterns*

Figure A.2 shows an example of a postal code pattern for France. In the case of England, the *territory code* is not used to calculate the postal code, consequently the depth level is fixed at zero (Figure A.3).

Figure A.2. *Example of a Postal Code Pattern for France*

---

2. Orchestra Networks' Model-driven MDM, EBX Platform.

Figure A.3. *Example of Territory Code for England*

Figure A.4 shows an example of the *postal code pattern* for France. In the case of England, the *postal code* is structured around four types of *Territory Office* (Figure A.5).

Figure A.4. *Example of country and postal code pattern for France*

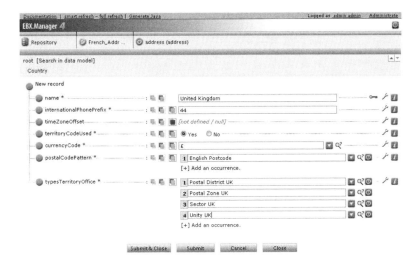

Figure A.5. *Example of Postal Code for England*

A.2.2. *Automatic calculation of postal code*

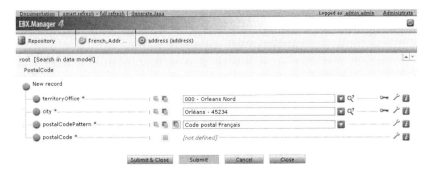

Figure A.6a. *Example of calculation of Postal Code for France*

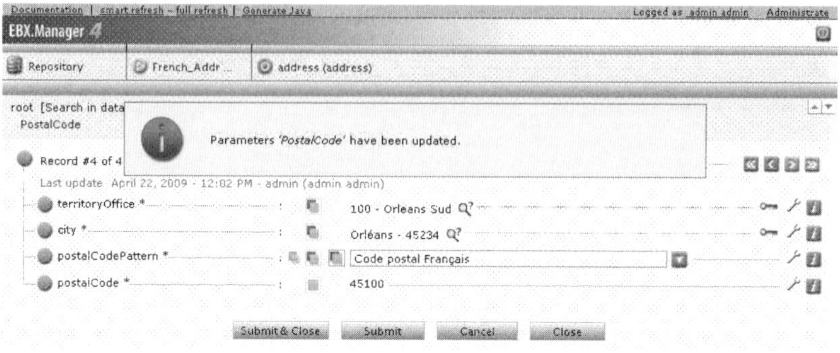

Figure A.6b. *Example of calculation of Postal Code for France*

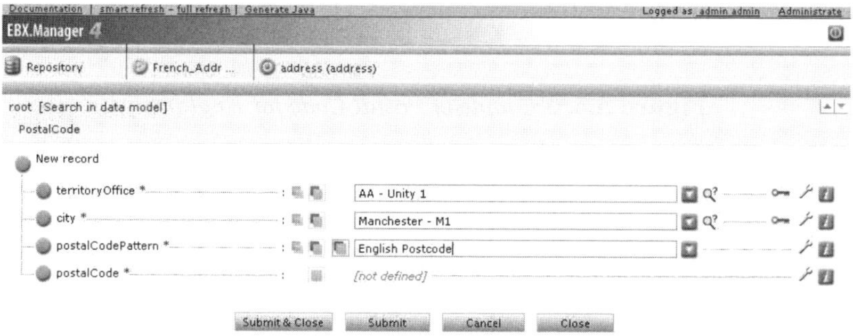

a)

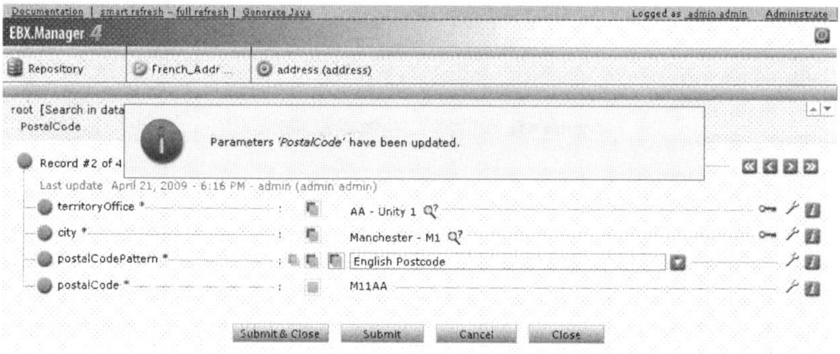

b)

Figures A.7a and b. *Example of Postal Code calculation for England*

A.2.3. Address input

Figure A.8. *Example of address input for France*

Figure A.9. *Example of address input for England*

A.3. Semantic modeling and data quality

The modeling that we have described considerably increases the data quality of addresses, as soon as the data has been input into the system. Due to the fact that each address is attached to an abstract *Object*, the identification of which is unified across the whole Information System without duplication, the risks of creating a duplicate address disappear. Unlike quality tools that clean up existing databases, semantic modeling establishes a new repository, the quality of which is fully enforced as soon as the data is initialized and updated.

The usual quality tools are still useful to clean up certain residual imperfections that can occur at the time of data input, but more simply, by acting on the MDM repository rather than legacy databases.

A.4. Performance

The response times to read an address in the MDM repository depend on the tool used. The indexing and optimization mechanisms enable creation of indexed views which collect, virtually, several semantic classes in the same logical table. The cohabitation between Model-driven MDM and classic OLTP databases is common. From then on, the data governance applied to address management is carried out in the MDM repository to then be injected into the OLTP databases that use them. In all cases, the MDM system remains the reference (one version of the truth) that influences all other systems (see also Chapter 12).

A.5. Lifecycle of the *Address* business object

The *Address* semantic class contains a set of extended business operations stemming from its state machine that defined its lifecycle. We have already described this dynamic aspect of modeling in detail with the presentation of the state machine Address in Chapter 9.

A.6. Insight into the XML schema

The XML schema below presents the *Postal Code* class, i.e. the associative class between *Territory Office* and *City*. It is easy to distinguish two foreign keys and the "/postal code" derived attribute, the business rule of which is attached in the model in the form of a declaration towards a Java class. When using a BRMS, calling on the rules engine would be at our disposal, which would avoid a hard-coded rule in Java programming language.

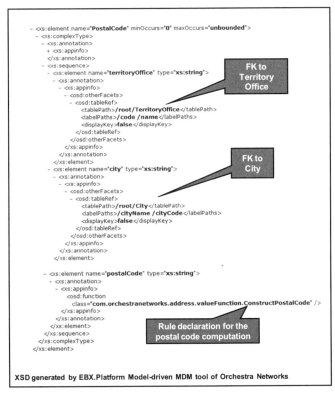

Figure A.10. *Example of XML schema with Postal Code*

This XML schema is generated from data logical modeling, and it is given to the MDM system which exploits it to automatically generate the user interface for the governance of addresses.

Bibliography

[AMA 05] AMAKO K., GIANI S., FOLGER G., *Geant4 User's Documents*,http://geant4.web.cern.ch/geant4/G4UsersDocuments/UsersGuides/ForApplicationDeveloper/html/Fundamentals/classCategory.html, 2005.

[BET 01] BETTS M., "Dirty Data", *ComputerWorld*, 17 December 2001.

[BON 09] BONNET P., DETAVERNIER J.-M., VAUQUIER D., *Sustainable IT Architecture*, ISTE, London, John Wiley and Sons, New York, 2009.

[BOO 94] BOOCH G., *Object-Oriented Analysis and Design*, Addison Wesley, London, UK, 1994.

[DEB 04] DEBAECKER D., *PLM, la gestion collaborative du cycle de vie des produits* (Product Life-cycle Management), Hermes, Paris, 2004.

[DUT 07] DUTTA S., BERGER R., *Recognising the True Value of Software Assets*, INSEAD School, 2007.

[ECK 01] ECKERSON W.-W., "Data Quality and the Bottom Line", Data Warehousing Institute (TDWI), 2001.

[FER 08] FERGUSON M., "Intelligent Business Strategies, Getting Started With Master Data Management", White paper, 2008.

[FOW 96] FOWLER M., *Analysis Patterns: Reusable Object Models*, Addison Wesley, London, UK, 1996.

[HOW 09] HOWARD P., "Data Discovery", White paper, Blooch Research, 2009.

[REG 08] REGNIER-PECASTING F., GABASSI M., FINET J., *MDM Enjeux et méthodes de la gestion des données*, Dunod, Paris, 2008.

[ROH 02] ROHM & HASS, "Laying the Groundwork for ERP: The story behind the company's Master Data", http://www.rohmhaas.com/formula/july2002/erp1.html, July 2002.

[RUS 08] RUSSOM P., "Defining Master Data Management", http://portals.tdwi.org, 2008.

[SIL 01] SILVERSTON L., "The Data Model Resource Book", in *A Library of Universal Data Models for All Companies* (vol.1), Second Edition, John Wiley and Son, New York, USA, 2001.

Index